Table of Contents

Table of Contents

Name: ______________________

Vocabulary: Synonyms

A **synonym** is a word that means the same, or nearly the same, as another word.
Example: quick and **fast**

Directions: Draw lines to match the words in Column A with their synonyms in Column B.

Column A	Column B
plain	unusual
career	vocation
rare	disappear
vanish	greedy
beautiful	finish
selfish	simple
complete	lovely

Directions: Choose a word from Column A or Column B to complete each sentence below.

1. Dad was very excited when he discovered the ______________ coin for sale on the display counter.

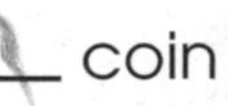

2. My dog is a real magician; he can ______________ into thin air when he sees me getting his bath ready!

3. Many of my classmates joined the discussion about ______________ choices we had considered.

4. "You will need to ______________ your report on ancient Greece before you sign up for computer time," said Mr. Rastetter.

5. Your ______________ painting will be on display in the art show.

Name: ____________________

Vocabulary: Synonyms

Directions: For each sentence, choose a word from the box that is a synonym for the bold word. Write the synonym above the word.

1. Boy, this road is really **bumpy**!

2. The operator said politely, "One **moment**, please."

3. My parents are usually **exhausted** when they get home from work.

4. "Don't be so **selfish**! Can't you share with us?" asked Rob.

5. That puzzle was actually quite **simple**.

6. "Who's your **buddy**?" Dad asked as we walked onto the porch.

7. When it comes to animals, my Uncle Steve is quite **intelligent**.

8. The frozen treat **thawed** while I stood in line for the bus.

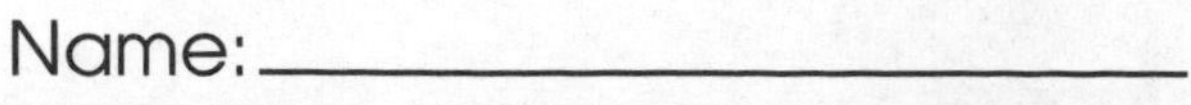

Name: ____________________

Vocabulary: Synonyms

Directions: For each paragraph, choose a word from the box that is a synonym for each bold word. Write the synonym above the word.

manual	beautiful	simple	wonderful	greatest	finished

Danielle and Mackenzie worked hard to earn the **best** badge for Girl Scouts. Each knew that her **workbook** had to be **completed** by the meeting on Saturday. Danielle's mother suggested that they work at the park and change it from a **plain** setting to something more **lovely**. The girls agreed that Danielle's mother had a **great** idea to help them earn the environmental badge.

beside	tired	evening	important	competition	hopped

The two boys **jumped** on their bikes and headed down the hill toward the park. Corey and Justin knew that they needed to be at ball practice today or they would be unable to play in the **game** Friday **night**. They had worked all day in the fields **alongside** their father. They were **exhausted**, but knew that it was **crucial** that they not be late.

Name: ______________________

Vocabulary: Antonyms

An **antonym** is a word that means the opposite of another word.
Example: difficult and **easy**

Directions: Choose words from the box to complete the crossword puzzle.

friend	vanish	quit	safety	liquids	scatter	help	noisy

ACROSS:

2. Opposite of **gather**
3. Opposite of **enemy**
4. Opposite of **prevent**
6. Opposite of **begin**
7. Opposite of **silent**

DOWN:

1. Opposite of **appear**
2. Opposite of **danger**
5. Opposite of **solids**

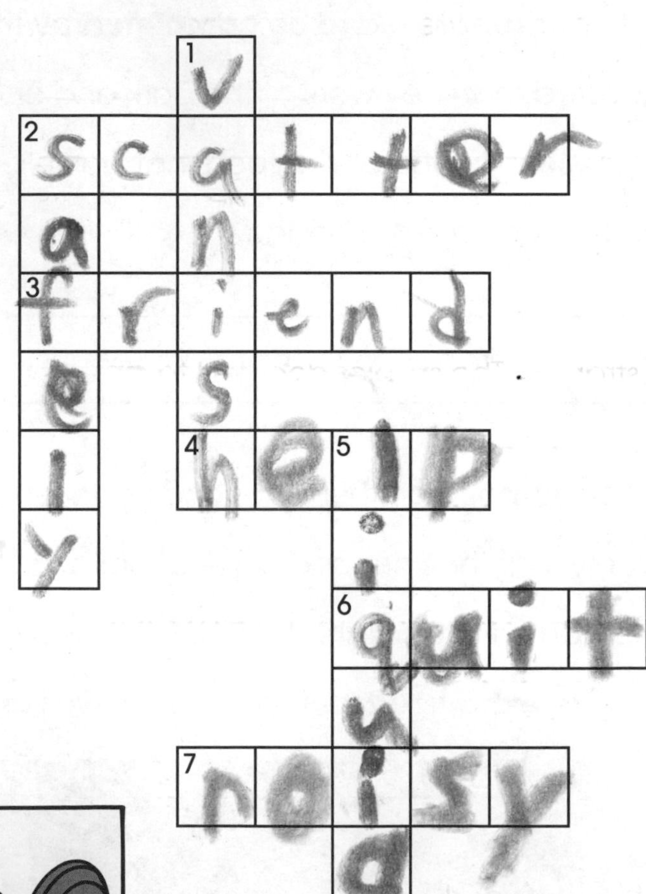

Name: ______________________

Vocabulary: Antonyms

Directions: Each bold word below has an antonym in the box. Use these words to write new sentences. The first one is done for you.

friend	vanish	quit	safety	liquids	help	scatter	worse

1. I'll help you **gather** all the papers on the lawn.
   The strong winds will scatter the leaves.
2. The fourth graders were learning about the many **solids** in their classroom.
   ____
3. "It's time to **begin** our lesson on the continents," said Ms. Haynes.
   ____
4. "That's strange. The stapler decided to **appear** all of a sudden," said Mr. Jonson.
   ____
5. The doctor said this new medicine should **prevent** colds.
   ____
6. "She is our **enemy**, boys, we can't let her in our clubhouse!" cried Paul.
   ____
7. I'm certain that dark cave is full of **danger**!
   ____
8. Give me a chance to make the situation **better**.
   ____

Name: ____________________

Vocabulary: Synonyms and Antonyms

Directions: Use the words in the box to write a synonym for each word below. Write it next to the S. Next to the A, write an antonym. The first one is done for you.

appear	proud	merry	straight	repair	plain
under	melted	unnecessary	late	new	smooth
embarrassed	gloomy	bent	break	fancy	above
icy	valuable	immediate	old	bumpy	vanish

1. crooked
   S: bent
   A: straight

2. frozen
   S: ____________
   A: ____________

3. instant
   S: ____________
   A: ____________

4. damage
   S: ____________
   A: ____________

5. important
   S: ____________
   A: ____________

6. ashamed
   S: ____________
   A: ____________

7. cheerful
   S: ____________
   A: ____________

8. elegant
   S: ____________
   A: ____________

9. rough
   S: ____________
   A: ____________

10. beneath
    S: ____________
    A: ____________

11. disappear
    S: ____________
    A: ____________

12. ancient
    S: ____________
    A: ____________

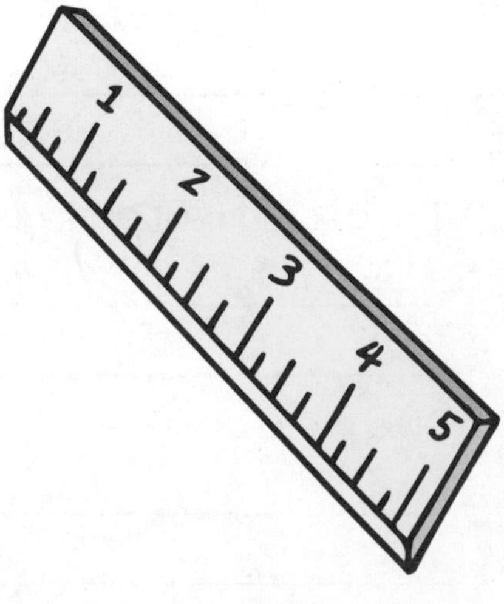

Name: ____________________

Vocabulary: Homophones

Homophones are two words that sound the same, have different meanings and are usually spelled differently.
Example: write and **right**

Directions: Write the correct homophone in each sentence below.

weight — how heavy something is
wait — to be patient

threw — tossed
through — passing between

steal — to take something that doesn't belong to you
steel — a heavy metal

1. Tho bands marched ____________ the streets lined with many cheering people.
2. ____________ for me by the flagpole.
3. One of our strict rules at school is: Never ____________ from another person.
4. Could you estimate the ____________ of this bowling ball?
5. The bleachers have ____________ rods on both ends and in the middle.
6. He walked in the door and ____________ his jacket down.

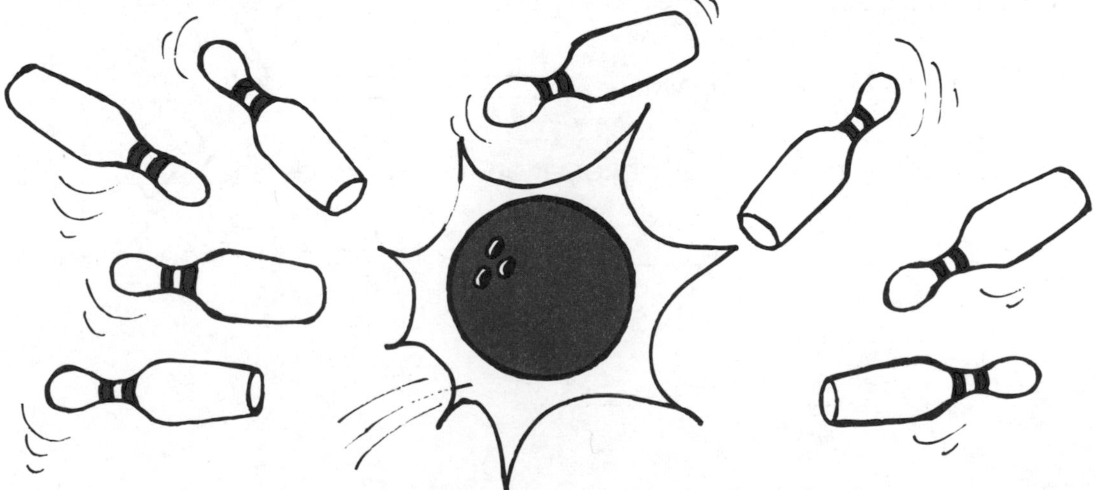

Name: ____________________

Vocabulary: Homophones

Directions: Write the correct homophone in each sentence below.

cent — a coin having the value of one penny
scent — odor or aroma

chews — grinds with the teeth
choose — to select

course — the path along which something moves
coarse — rough in texture

heard — received sounds in the ear
herd — a group of animals

1. My uncle Mike always ____________________ each bite of his food 20 times!
2. As we walked through her garden, we detected the ________________ of roses.
3. It was very peaceful sitting on the hillside watching the ____________________ of cattle grazing.
4. Which flavor of ice cream did you ____________________?
5. The friendly clerk let me buy the jacket even though I was one ______________ short.
6. You will need ____________________ sandpaper to make the wood smoother.

Name: ______________________

Vocabulary: Words That Sound Alike

Directions: Choose the correct word in parentheses to complete each sentence. The first one is done for you.

1. Jimmy was so ___bored___ that he fell asleep. (board, bored)
2. We'll need a ______________ and some nails to repair the fence. (board, bored)
3. Do you want ______________ after dinner? (desert, dessert)
4. A ______________ is hot and sandy. (desert, dessert)
5. The soldier had a ______________ pinned to his uniform. (medal, metal)
6. Gold is a precious ______________ . (medal, metal)
7. Don't ______________ at your present before Christmas! (peak, peek)
8. They climbed to the ______________ of the mountain. (peak, peek)
9. Jack had to repair the emergency ______________ on his car. (brake, break)
10. Please be careful not to ______________ my bicycle. (brake, break)
11. The race ______________ was a very difficult one. (coarse, course)
12. We will need some ______________ sandpaper to finish the job. (coarse, course)

Name: ____________________

Vocabulary: Prefixes

A **prefix** is a syllable at the beginning of a word that changes its meaning.

Directions: Add a prefix to the beginning of each word in the box to make a word with the meaning given in each sentence below. The first one is done for you.

PREFIX	MEANING
bi	two or twice
en	to make
in	within
mis	wrong
non	not or without
pre	before
re	again
un	not

grown   write   information   large   cycle   usual   school   sense

1. Jimmy's foot hurt because his toenail was (growing within). ingrown
2. If you want to see what is in the background, you will have to (make bigger) the photograph. ____________
3. I didn't do a very good job on my homework, so I will have to (write it again) it. ____________
4. The newspaper article about the event has some (wrong facts). ____________
5. I hope I get a (vehicle with two wheels) for my birthday. ____________
6. The story he told was complete (words without meaning)! ____________
7. Did you go to (school that comes before kindergarten) before you went to kindergarten? ____________
8. The ability to read words upside down is most (not usual). ____________

Name: ______________________

Vocabulary: Prefixes

Directions: Circle the correct word for each sentence.

1. You will need to ______________ the directions before you complete this page.

   reset reread repair

2. Since she is allergic to milk products she has to

   use ______________ products.

   nondairy nonsense nonmetallic

3. That certainly was an ______________ costume he selected for the Halloween party.

   untied unusual unable

4. The directions on the box said to ____________ the oven before baking the brownies.

   preheat preschool prevent

5. "I'm sorry if I ____________ you as to the cost of the trip," explained the travel agent.

   misdialed misread misinformed

6. You may use the overhead projector to ______________ the picture so the whole class can see it.

   enlarge enable endanger

Name: 

Vocabulary: Suffixes

A **suffix** is a syllable at the end of a word that changes its meaning. In most cases, when adding a suffix that begins with a vowel, drop the final **e** of the root word. For example, **fame** becomes **famous**. Also, change a final **y** in the root word to **i** before adding any suffix except **ing**. For example, **silly** becomes **silliness**.

Directions: Add a suffix to the end of each word in the box to make a word with the meaning given (in parentheses) in each sentence below. The first one is done for you.

SUFFIX	MEANING
ful	full of
ity	quality or degree
ive	have or tend to be
less	without or lacking
able	able to be
ness	state of
ment	act of
or	person that does something
ward	in the direction of

effect like thought pay beauty thank back act happy

1. Mike was (full of thanksl) for a hot meal. thankful
2. I was (without thinking) for forgetting your birthday. ________
3. The mouse trap we put out doesn't seem to be (have an effect). ________
4. In spring, the flower garden is (full of beauty). ________
5. Sally is such a (able to be liked) girl! ________
6. Tim fell over (in the direction of the back) because he wasn't watching where he was going. ________
7. Jill's wedding day was one of great (the state of being happy). ________
8. The (person who performs) was very good in the play. ________
9. I have to make a (act of paying) for the stereo I bought. ________

Name: ____________________

Vocabulary: Suffixes

Directions: Read the story. Choose the correct word from the box to complete the sentences.

beautiful	colorful	payment
breakable	careful	backward
careless	director	agreement
basement	forward	firmness

Colleen and Marj carried the boxes down to the ______________ apartment. "Be ______________ with those," cautioned Colleen's mother. "All the things in that box are ______________." As soon as the two girls helped carry all the boxes from the moving van down the stairs, they would be able to go to school for the play tryouts. That was the ______________ made with Colleen's mother earlier that day.

"It won't do any good to get ______________ with your work. Just keep at it and the job will be done quickly," she spoke with a ______________ in her voice.

"It's hard to see where I'm going when I have to walk ______________," groaned Marj. "Can we switch places with the next box?"

Colleen agreed to switch places, but they soon discovered that the last two boxes were lightweight. Each girl had her own box to carry, so each of them got to walk looking ______________. "These are so light," remarked Marj. "What's in them?"

"These have the ______________, ______________ hats I was telling you about. We can take them to the play tryouts with us," answered Colleen. "I bet we'll impress the ______________. Even if we don't get parts in the play, I bet our hats will!"

Colleen's mother handed each of the girls a 5-dollar bill. "I really appreciate your help. Will this be enough?"

"Thanks, Mom. You bet!" Colleen shouted as the girls ran down the sidewalk.

Name: ____________________

Vocabulary: Parts of the Body

Directions: Unscramble the remaining letters of each word that names a part of the body. Then write each word in the sentence that describes it. The first one is done for you.

anirb b__________

noteug t__________

rilev l__________

skidyen k__________

gluns l__________

erath h__________

shoctam s__________

Your brain is the part of your body you think with.

They help clean your blood. __________

Your __________ helps to digest food after it is swallowed.

Your __________ makes a liquid that helps you to digest your food.

Your __________ pumps blood throughout your body with each beat.

Your __________ are filled with air when you breathe.

Your __________ is the muscle in your mouth that helps you talk and taste.

Name: ____________________

Vocabulary: Occupations

Directions: Unscramble the bold words to write the title of the person who does the described job. The first one is done for you.

1. A **inacimus** writes, sings or plays music. musician
2. An **trasotanu** is trained to fly a spaceship. ____________
3. An **itrode** prepares other people's writing to be printed in a book, newspaper or magazine. ____________
4. An **rigeenen** operates an engine, such as on a train. ____________
5. An **brocata** performs gymnastic or tumbling exercises that use control of the body. ____________

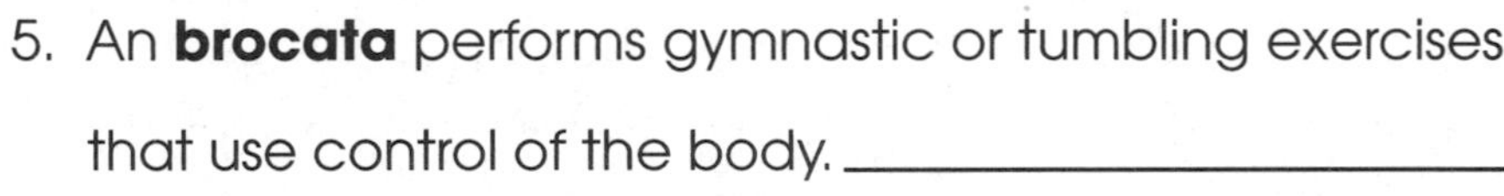

6. A **ilaort** makes clothing for people. ____________
7. A **veecitted** works to get information, especially about crimes or suspicious people. ____________
8. A **tissicent** works and performs experiments in one of the sciences, such as chemistry. ____________
9. An **sattir** makes beautiful things, such as paintings and statues. ____________
10. A **hocca** teaches and trains students, especially in sports. ____________
11. An **rotac** performs in plays or movies. ____________
12. A **suner** is trained to care for sick people and to assist doctors. ____________
13. A **naicigam** is a performer skilled in magic tricks. ____________

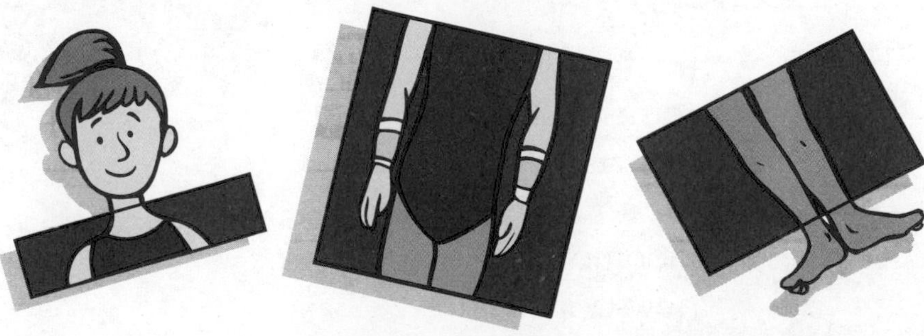

Name: ____________________

Vocabulary: Occupations

Directions: Find each word from the box in the word search and circle it. Words may go across, down, diagonal or backward.

magician scientist coach astronaut musician acrobat tailor
engineer nurse detective actor artist editor

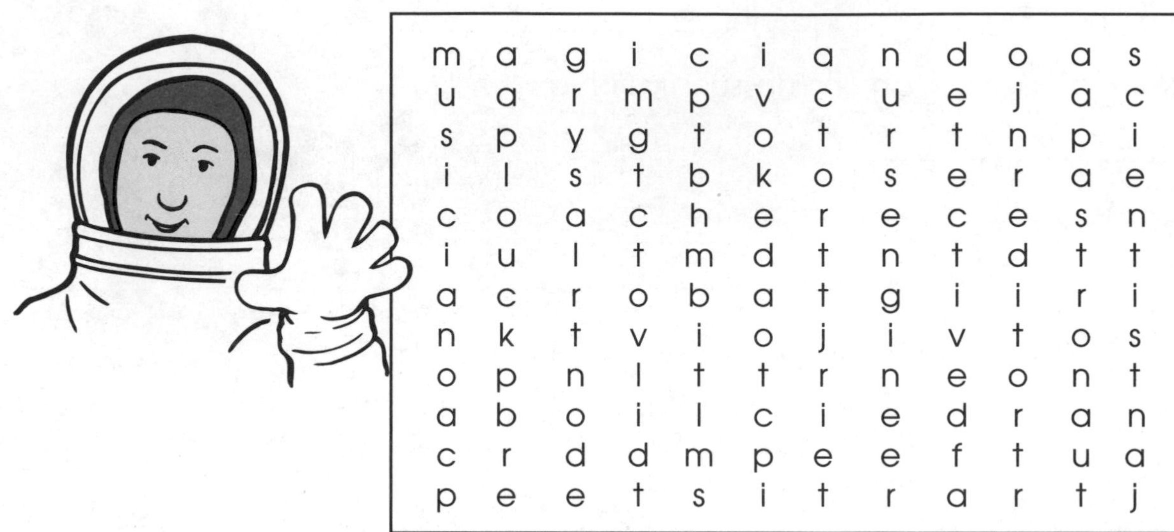

Directions: Draw a line between each job and the word that best goes with it.

actor	wand
tailor	basketball
acrobat	painting
astronaut	guitar
coach	medicine
editor	telescope
scientist	stage
magician	mystery
artist	somersault
nurse	scissors
engineer	rocket
musician	locomotive
detective	newspaper

Name: ____________________

Vocabulary: Sports

Directions: Find each word in the word search. Then unscramble the bold words in the sentences below.

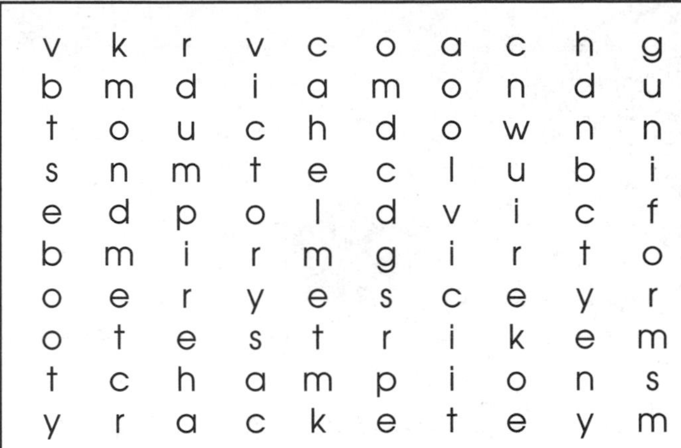

champion
helmet
diamond
strike
uniforms
touchdown
umpire
coach
club
victory
racket

1. A football player wears a **melteh** to protect his head. ____________________
2. If our team wins tonight, it will be our tenth **rticoyv** this year. ____________________
3. When it rained, they put a cover over the baseball **middona**. ____________________
4. Our **hacco** asked us to stay after school to practice . ____________________
5. With only a minute left in the football game, Jimmy scored the winning

   wontcudoh. ____________________
6. In golf, you hit the ball with a **bluc**. ____________________
7. Do all boxing fans know the name of the heavy-weight **miocpahn**? ____________________
8. I thought I tagged the base, but the **mipure** said I was out. ____________________
9. In tennis, you hit the ball with a **rcatek**. ____________________
10. If we earn enough money selling candy, our team will get new

    nifmorus. ____________________
11. I bet our best pitcher can **trekis** out your best hitter. ____________________

Name: 

Reading Skills: Context Clues

When you read, you may confuse words that look alike. You can tell when you read a word incorrectly because it doesn't make sense. You can tell from the **context** (the other words in the sentence or the sentences before or after) what the word should be. These **context clues** can help you figure out the meaning of a word by relating it to other words in the sentence.

Directions: Circle the correct word for each sentence below. Use the context to help you.

1. We knew we were in trouble as soon as we heard the crash.

   The baseball had gone (through, thought) the picture window!

2. She was not able to answer my question because her (month, mouth) was full of pizza.
3. Asia is the largest continent in the (world, word).
4. I'm not sure I heard the teacher correctly. Did he say what I (through, thought) he said?
5. I was not with them on vacation so I don't know a (think, thing) about what happened.
6. My favorite (month, mouth) of the year is July because I love fireworks and parades!
7. You will do better on your book report if you (think, thing) about what you are going to say.

Name: ____________________

Reading Skills: Context Clues

Directions: Read each sentence carefully and circle the word that makes sense.

1. We didn't (except, expect) you to arrive so early.
2. "I can't hear a (word, world) you are saying. Wait until I turn down the stereo," said Val.
3. I couldn't sleep last night because of the (noise, nose) from the apartment below us.
4. Did Peggy say (weather, whether) or not we needed our binoculars for the game?
5. He broke his (noise, nose) when he fell off the bicycle.
6. All the students (except, expect) the four in the front row are excused to leave.
7. The teacher said we should have good (whether, weather) for our field trip.

Directions: Choose a word pair from the sentences above to write two sentences of your own.

1. ____

____

2. ____

____

Name: ______________________

Reading Skills: Context Clues

Directions: Use context clues to figure out the bold word in each sentence below.

1. The teacher wanted all of us to put the names of the students in our class in two **columns**. It was a big help when I saw how she started each list on the board.
2. "I'm glad to see such a **variety** of art projects at the display," said the principal. "I was afraid that many of the projects would be the same."
3. My father used to work for a huge **corporation** in Florida. Since we moved to Virginia, his job is with a smaller company.
4. It would be hard to come up with a **singular** reason for the football team's success. There are so many good things happening that could explain it.

Directions: Draw a line to match the word on the left with its definition on the right.

variety	one
corporation	a large business
columns	vertical listings
singular	many different kinds

Name: ____________________

Reading Skills: Context Clues

Directions: Use context clues to help you choose the correct word for each sentence below.

selected	match	scarecrow

Diane and Donna are twin sisters. The clothes they wear nearly always ________________ . At school one day, Donna's teacher ________________ one of the students to dress up as a scarecrow for the fall harvest play. She chose Donna. Everyone was quite surprised the night of the play. Donna was not the only ________________ . Diane looked the part, too!

problem	driver	intersection

Dad sometimes works very late. This caused a ________________ on his way home last night. As he was approaching the ________________ near our home, he started to fall asleep! The whole family was very glad that the ________________ in the car behind Dad honked his car horn to wake him up.

cancel	decision	storm

"It looks very much like it could ________________ tonight," said Brent. Rob replied, "Are you saying we should ________________ our game?" "Let's not make a ________________ just yet," answered Brent.

Name: ____________________

Reading Skills: Context Clues

Directions: Use context clues to help you choose the correct word for each sentence below.

designs	studying	collection

Our fourth-grade class will be ____________________ castles for the next four weeks. Mrs. Oswalt will be helping with our study. She plans to share her ____________________ of castle models with the class. We are all looking forward to our morning in the sand at the school's volleyball court. We all get to try our own ____________________ to see how they work.

breath	excited	quietly

Michelle was very ________________ the other day when she came into the classroom. We all noticed that she had trouble sitting ________________ in her seat until it was her turn to share with us. When her turn finally came, she took a deep ________________ and told us that her mom was going to have a baby!

responsibility	chooses	messages

Each week, our teacher ________________ classroom helpers. They get to be part of the Job Squad. Some helpers have the ________________ of watering the plants. Everyone's favorite job is when they get to take ________________ to the office or to another teacher's room.

Name: ______________________

Reading Skills: Context Clues

Directions: Read the story. Match each bold word with its definition below.

Where the northern shores of North America meet the Arctic Ocean, the winters are very long and cold. No plants or crops will grow there. This is the land of the **Eskimo**.

Eskimos have figured out ways to live in the snow and ice. They sometimes live in **igloos**, which are made of snow. It is really very comfortable inside! An oil lamp provides light and warmth.

Often, you will find a big, furry **husky** sleeping in the long tunnel that leads to the igloo. Huskies are very important to Eskimos because they pull their sleds and help with hunting. Eskimos are excellent hunters. Many, many years ago they learned to make **harpoons** and spears to help them hunt their food.

Eskimos get much of their food from the sea, especially fish, seals and whales. Often, an Eskimo will go out in a **kayak** to fish. Only one Eskimo fits inside, and he drives it with a paddle. The waves may turn the kayak upside down, but the Eskimo does not fall out. He is so skillful with a paddle that he quickly is right side up again.

A ______________________ is a large, strong dog.

An ______________________ is a member of the race of people who live on the Arctic coasts of North America and in parts of Greenland.

______________________ are houses made of packed snow.

A ______________________ is a one-person canoe made of animal skins.

______________________ are spears with a long rope attached. They are used for spearing whales and other large sea animals.

Name: ____________________

Reading Skills: Context Clues

Directions: In each sentence below, circle the correct meaning for the nonsense word.

1. Be careful when you put that plate back on the shelf—it is **quibbable**.

   flexible   colorful   breakable

2. What is your favorite kind of **tonn**, pears or bananas?

   fruit   salad   purple

3. The **dinlay** outside this morning was very chilly; I needed my sweater.

   tree   vegetable   temperature

4. The whole class enjoyed the **weat**. They wanted to see it again next Friday.

   colorful   plant   video

5. Ashley's mother brought in a **zundy** she made by hand.

   temperature   quilt   plant

6. "Why don't you sit over here, Ronnie? That **sloey** is not very comfortable," said Mr. Gross.

   chair   car   cat

Name: ____________________

Reading Skills: Context Clues

Directions: In each sentence below, circle the correct meaning for the nonsense word.

1. The girls all liked their soccer **riftale**. She taught them how to be a real team.

   ball coach potato

2. I loved your painting at the school **dif** show!

   fan automobile art

3. Everyone returned their permission **rihs** on time, so they all got to go on the field trip.

   fruits slips teachers

4. The teacher said, "Please open your science **powts** to chapter six."

   books kits cactus

5. The school picnic had to be cancelled because of the **poledak**.

   sky storm automobile

6. Mother put the quarters into the parking **ait** while I got my things from the car.

   headset garage meter

7. This time of year the leaves on the trees look so **bufamvy**.

   colorful sad tired

Name: 

Reading Skills: Classifying

Classifying is placing similar things into categories.

Directions: Classify each group by crossing out the word that does not belong.

1. factory hotel lodge pattern
2. Thursday September December October
3. cottage hut carpenter castle
4. cupboard orchard refrigerator stove
5. Christmas Thanksgiving Easter spring
6. brass copper coal tin
7. stomach breathe liver brain
8. teacher mother dentist office
9. musket faucet bathtub sink
10. basement attic kitchen neighborhood

Name: 

Reading Skills: Classifying

Directions: Choose a word or phrase from the box that describes each group below.

color words	vegetables	gems
explorers	metals	vehicles
things that fly	insects	

1. ____________________
   a. hot-air balloons
   b. jets
   c. bi-planes

2. ____________________
   a. iron
   b. gold
   c. copper

3. ____________________
   a. ruby
   b. diamond
   c. emerald

4. ____________________
   a. magenta
   b. green
   c. black

5. ____________________
   a. Ponce de Leon
   b. Lewis and Clark
   c. Magellan

6. ____________________
   a. beets
   b. carrots
   c. asparagus

7. ____________________
   a. mosquito
   b. cricket
   c. ant

8. ____________________
   a. mini-van
   b. bus
   c. convertible

Name: ____________________

Reading Skills: Classifying

Directions: Read the title of each TV show. Write the correct number to tell what kind of show it is.

1 — Cooking	3 — Sports	5 — Humor
2 — Nature	4 — Mystery	6 — Famous People

______ *The Secret of the Lost Locket*

______ *Learn Tennis With the Pros*

______ *Birds in the Wild*

______ *The Life of George Washington*

______ *Great Recipes From Around the World*

______ *A Laugh a Minute*

Directions: Read the description of each TV show. Write the number of each show above in the blank.

______ The years before he became the first president of the United States are examined.

______ Featured: eagles and owls

______ Clues lead Detective Logan to a cemetery in his search for the missing necklace.

______ Famous players give tips on buying a racket.

______ Six ways to cook chicken

______ Cartoon characters in short stories

Name: ______________________

Reading Skills: Classifying

Directions: Complete each idea by crossing out the word or phrase that does not belong.

1. If the main idea is **things that are green**, I don't need:

   the sun apples grass leaves in summer

2. If the idea is **musical instruments**, I don't need a:

   piano trombone beach ball tuba

3. If the idea is **months of the year**, I don't need:

   Friday January July October

4. If the idea is **colors on the U.S. flag**, I don't need:

   white blue black red

5. If the idea is **types of weather**, I don't need:

   sleet stormy roses sunny

6. If the idea is **fruits**, I don't need:

   kiwi orange spinach banana

7. If the idea is **U.S. presidents**, I don't need:

   Lincoln Jordan Washington Adams

8. If the idea is **flowers**, I don't need:

   oak daisy tulip daffodil

9. If the idea is **sports**, I don't need:

   pears soccer wrestling baseball

Name: ______________________

Reading Skills: Classifying

Directions: Read the Story. Find words in the story that belong in the lists below. Write the words under the correct lists.

Meg, Joey and Ryan are talking about what they want to do when they grow up. Meg says, "I want to be a great writer. I'll write lots of books, and articles for newspapers and magazines."

"I want to be a famous athlete," says Joey. "I'll play baseball in the summer and football in the fall."

"Oh, yes," adds Meg. "I want to be a famous tennis star, too. When I'm not busy writing books, I'll play in tournaments all over the world. I'll be the world's champion!"

Ryan says, "That sounds pretty good. But I think I'll be a doctor and a carpenter. I'll build my very own cabin that I can live in during the winter."

"I'm going to live in a lighthouse by the sea," says Joey. "I've always wanted to do that. Then I can go fishing any time I want."

"I suppose I'll live in a castle when I grow up," says Meg. "World champion tennis players make lots of money!"

Jobs

1. ______________________
2. ______________________
3. ______________________
4. ______________________

Sports

1. ______________________
2. ______________________
3. ______________________
4. ______________________

Seasons

1. ______________________
2. ______________________
3. ______________________

Houses

1. ______________________
2. ______________________
3. ______________________

Name: ____________________

Reading Skills: Analogies

An **analogy** is a way of comparing things to show how they are similar.

Directions: Read the sentences below. Determine how the first pair of words is related. Complete the second pair that relates in the same way. The first one is done for you.

cut	carry	ran	arm	listen
paint	lie	children	50	out
puppy	summer	hot	water	egg

1. Pencil is to write as brush is to paint.
2. Foot is to leg as hand is to ____________________.
3. Crayons are to draw as scissors are to ____________________.
4. Leg is to walk as arm is to ____________________.
5. Baby is to babies as child is to ____________________.
6. Eye is to look as ear is to ____________________.
7. Chair is to sit as bed is to ____________________.
8. 600 is to 300 as 100 is to ____________________.
9. White is to black as in is to ____________________.
10. Ice skate is to winter as swim is to ____________________.
11. Switch is to light as faucet is to ____________________.
12. Fly is to flew as run is to ____________________.
13. Cow is to milk as chicken is to ____________________.
14. Cool is to cold as warm is to ____________________.
15. Cat is to kitten as dog is to ____________________.

Name: ____________________

Reading Skills: Analogies

Directions: Write a word from the box to complete the following analogies.

fence	club	glove	saw	father
blanket	dish	rug	snow	ten
compass	hat	brake	finger	blue

1. Racket is to tennis as ____________________ is to golf.
2. Glass is to drink as ____________________ is to eat.
3. Wheel is to steer as ____________________ is to stop.
4. Roof is to house as ____________________ is to floor.
5. Rain is to storm as ____________________ is to blizzard.
6. Clock is to time as ____________________ is to directions.
7. Lid is to pan as ____________________ is to head.
8. Hammer is to pound as ____________________ is to cut.
9. Mother is to daughter as ____________________ is to son.
10. Shoe is to foot as ____________________ is to hand.
11. Five is to ten as ____________________ is to twenty.
12. Shade is to lamp as ____________________ is to bed.
13. Toe is to foot as ____________________ is to hand.
14. Frame is to picture as ____________________ is to yard.
15. Green is to grass as ____________________ is to sky.

Name: 

Review

Directions: Complete the puzzle to review the words you have learned.

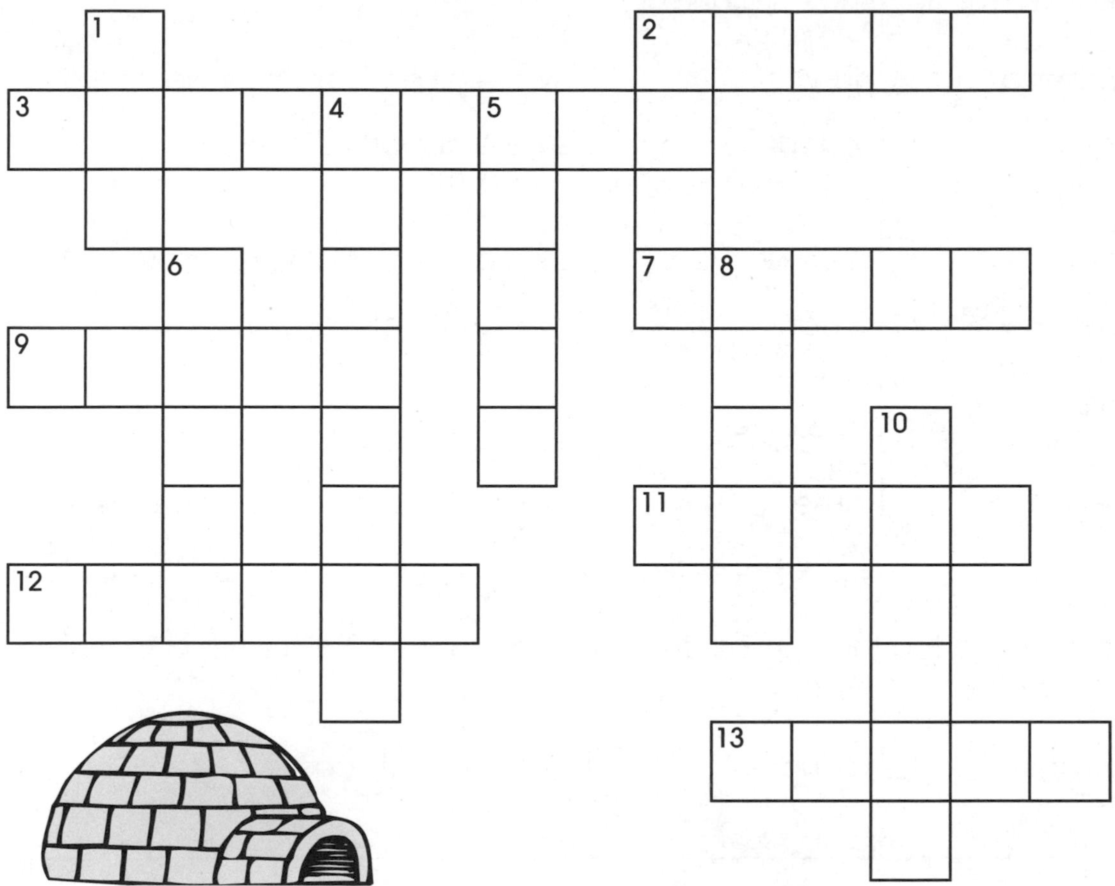

ACROSS:

2. An antonym for **fancy**
3. A person who solves crimes
7. A one-person canoe used by Eskimos
9. A person who cares for sick people and assists doctors
11. A homophone for **board**
12. A synonym for **disappear**
13. This pumps blood with every beat

DOWN:

1. An antonym for **old**
2. A homophone for **peak**
4. A root word plus a suffix that means "without care"
5. A snow house some Eskimos live in
6. You think with this
8. A person who performs in a movie or play
10. A prefix plus a root word that means "read again"

Name: ______________________

Review

Directions: Check the three words that belong together. Then draw a line under the sentence that tells how they are alike.

1. ☐ forehead ☐ jaw — They are all parts of the face.
   ☐ shoulder ☐ cheek — They are all parts of the arm.

2. ☐ collar ☐ sleeve — They are all parts of your body.
   ☐ cuff ☐ heart — They are all parts of a shirt.

3. ☐ camera ☐ trumpet — They are all used to make music.
   ☐ guitar ☐ flute — They are all used to take pictures.

Directions: Check the three words that belong together. Then write a sentence to tell how they are alike.

☐ cottage ☐ princess ☐ hut ☐ castle

____

____

Directions: Write a word to complete each analogy.

1. Car is to drive as ______________ is to fly.
2. Basement is to bottom as attic is to ______________ .
3. Calf is to cow as colt is to ______________ .
4. Bark is to dog as ______________ is to cow.
5. Laugh is to happy as ______________ is to sad.

Name: ____________________________

Following Directions: Maps

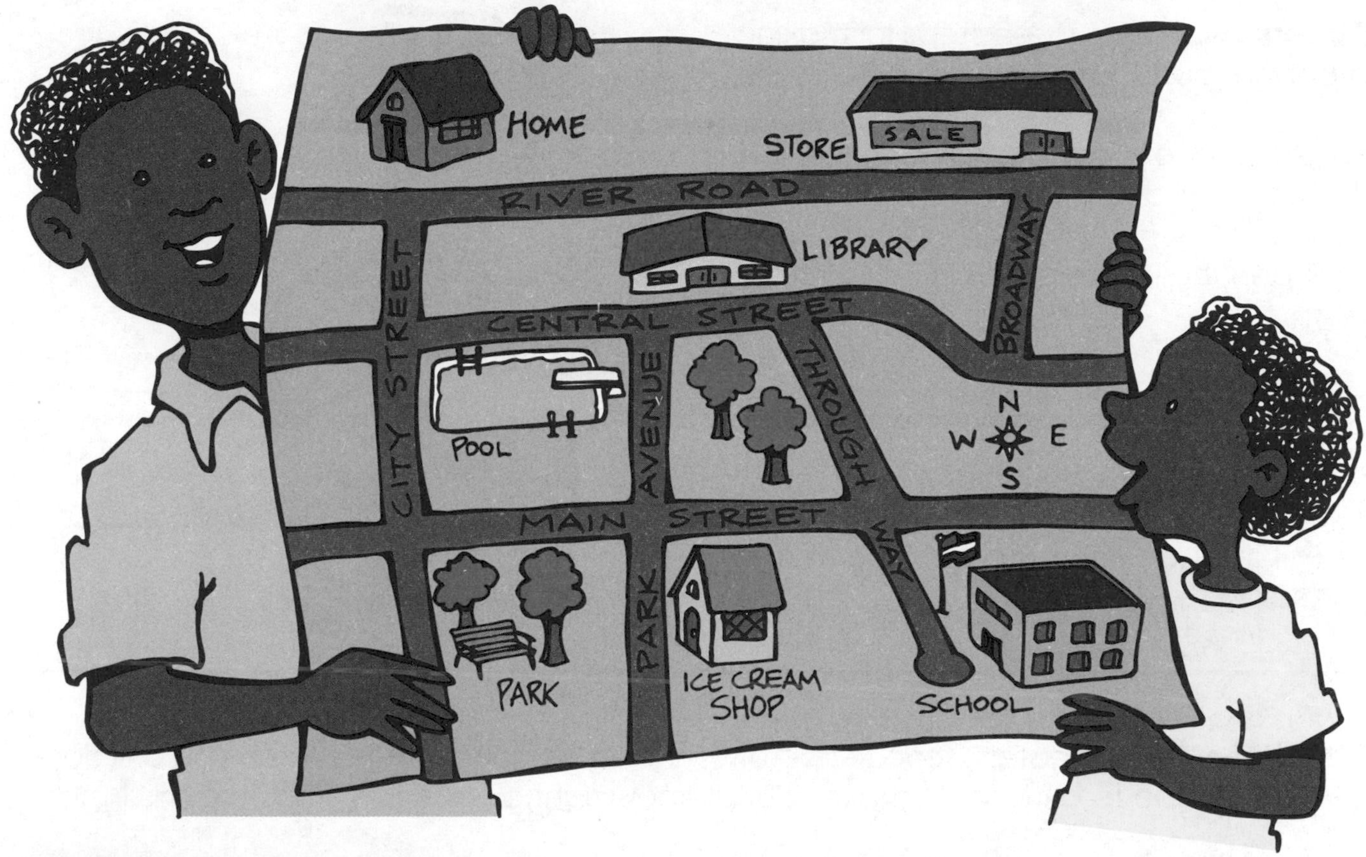

Directions: Follow the directions below to reach a "mystery" location on the map.

1. Begin at home.
2. Drive east on River Road.
3. Turn south on Broadway.
4. Drive to Central Street and turn west.
5. When you get to City Street, turn south.
6. Turn east on Main Street and drive one block to Park Avenue; turn north.
7. At Central Street turn east, then turn southeast on Through Way.
8. Drive to the end of Through Way. Your "mystery" location is to the east.

You are at the ____________________ .

Can you write an easier way to get back home?

____

____

____

Name: ____________

Following Directions: Recipes

Directions: Follow these steps for making a peanut butter and jelly sandwich.

1. Get a jar of peanut butter, a jar of jelly, two slices of bread and a knife.
2. Open the jar lids.
3. Using the knife, spread peanut butter on one slice of bread.
4. Spread jelly on the other slice of bread.
5. Put the two slices of bread together to make a sandwich.

Directions: Write the steps for a recipe of your own. Be very specific. When you are done, give the recipe to a friend to make. You will know right away if any steps are missing!

Recipe for: ____________________

1. ____________________
2. ____________________
3. ____________________
4. ____________________
5. ____________________
6. ____________________

Name: ____________________

Following Directions: Recipes

Sequencing is putting items or events in logical order.

Directions: Read the recipe. Then number the steps in order for making brownies.

Preheat the oven to 350 degrees. Grease an 8-inch square baking dish.

In a mixing bowl, place two squares (2 ounces) of unsweetened chocolate and 1/3 cup butter. Place the bowl in a pan of hot water and heat it to melt the chocolate and the butter.

When the chocolate is melted, remove the pan from the heat. Add 1 cup sugar and two eggs to the melted chocolate and beat it. Next, stir in 3/4 cup sifted flour, 1/2 teaspoon baking powder and 1/2 teaspoon salt. Finally, mix in 1/2 cup chopped nuts.

Spread the mixture in the greased baking dish. Bake for 30 to 35 minutes. The brownies are done when a toothpick stuck in the center comes out clean. Let the brownies cool. Cut them into squares.

________ Stick a toothpick in the center of the brownies to make sure they are done.

________ Mix in chopped nuts.

________ Melt chocolate and butter in a mixing bowl over a pan of hot water.

________ Cool brownies and cut into squares.

________ Beat in sugar and eggs.

________ Spread mixture in a baking dish.

________ Stir in flour, baking powder and salt.

________ Bake for 30 to 35 minutes.

________ Turn oven to 350 degrees and grease pan.

Name: ____________________

Following Directions: Salt Into Pepper

Directions: Read how to do a magic trick that will amaze your friends. Then number the steps in order to do the trick.

Imagine doing this trick for your friends. Pick up a salt shaker that everyone can see is full of salt. Pour some into your hand. Tell your audience that you will change the salt into pepper. Say a few magic words, such as "Fibbiddy, dibbiddy, milkshake and malt. What will be pepper once was salt!" Then open your hand and pour out pepper!

How is it done? First you need a clear salt shaker with a screw-on top. You also need a paper napkin and a small amount of pepper.

Take off the top of the salt shaker. Lay the napkin over the opening and push it down a little to make a small pocket. Fill the pocket with pepper. Put the top back on the salt shaker and tear off the extra napkin. Now you are ready for the trick.

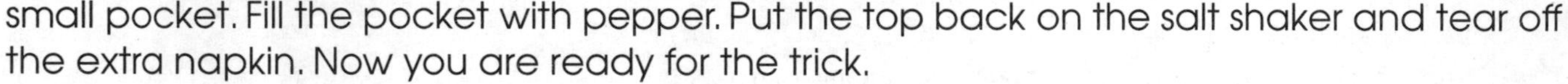

Hold up the salt shaker so your audience can see that it is full of salt. Shake some "salt" into your hand. Close your fist so no one can see that it is really pepper. Say the magic words and open your hand.

_______ Say some magic words.

_______ Find a clear salt shaker with a screw-on top.

_______ Open your hand and pour out the pepper.

_______ Take off the top of the salt shaker.

_______ Show the audience the shaker full of salt.

_______ Place the napkin over the opening of the salt shaker.

_______ Get a paper napkin and some pepper.

_______ Put the pepper in the napkin pocket.

_______ Shake some "salt" into your hand and close your fist.

_______ Put the top back on the salt shaker and tear off the extra napkin.

Name: ______________________

Following Directions: A Rocket Launcher

Directions: Read about how to make a rocket launcher. Then number the steps in order below. **Have an adult help you.**

Here's a science experiment that you can do in your own backyard. To make this rocket launcher, you need an empty 1-quart soda bottle, cork, paper towel, 1/2 cup water, 1/2 cup vinegar and 1 teaspoon baking soda. You may want to add some streamers.

The cork will be the rocket. If you attach tissue paper streamers to the cork with a thumbtack, you will be able to follow the rocket more easily during its flight.

Pour the water and vinegar into the launcher—the bottle. Cut the paper towel into a 4-inch square. Place the baking soda in the middle of the paper towel. Roll up the towel and twist the ends so the baking soda will stay inside.

Outside, where there will be plenty of room for the rocket to fly, drop the paper towel and baking soda into the bottle. Put the cork on as tightly as you can.

The liquid will soak through the paper towel. This lets the baking soda and vinegar work together to make a kind of gas called carbon dioxide. As the carbon dioxide builds up in the bottle, it will push out the cork. Soon the cork will shoot up into the sky with a loud pop!

_______ Pour the vinegar and water into the soda bottle.

_______ Attach streamers to the cork so you can follow its flight.

_______ Stand back and watch your rocket blast off!

_______ Place the baking soda on the paper towel and roll it up.

_______ Wait as the vinegar and baking soda work to make carbon dioxide gas.

_______ Drop the paper towel with the baking soda into the bottle.

_______ Gather together a bottle, cork, water, vinegar, paper towel and baking soda.

_______ Put on the cork as tightly as you can.

Name: ____________________

Reading Skills: Sequencing

Directions: Read each set of events. Then number them in the correct order.

_______ Get dressed for school and hurry downstairs for breakfast.

_______ Roll over, sleepy-eyed, and turn off the alarm clock.

_______ Meet your friends at the corner to walk to school.

_______ The fourth-grade class walked quietly to a safe area away from the building.

_______ The teacher reminded the last student to shut the classroom door.

_______ The loud clanging of the fire alarm startled everyone in the room.

_______ Barb's dad watched from the seat of the tractor as the boys and girls climbed into the wagon.

_______ By the time they returned to the barn, there wasn't much straw left.

_______ As the wagon bumped along the trail, the boys and girls sang songs they learned in music class.

_______ The referee blew his whistle and held up the hand of the winner of the match.

_______ Each wrestler worked hard, trying to out-maneuver his opponent.

_______ The referee said, "Shake hands, boys, and wrestle a fair match."

Name: ______________________

Reading Skills: Sequencing

Directions: In each group below, one event in the sequence is missing. Write the correct sentence from the box where it belongs.

- Paul put his bait on the hook and cast out into the pond.
- "Sorry," he said, "but the TV repairman can't get here until Friday."
- Everyone pitched in and helped.
- Corey put the ladder up against the trunk of the tree.

1. "All the housework has to be done before anyone goes to the game," said Mom.
2. ______________________
3. We all agreed that "many hands make light work."

1. ______________________
2. It wasn't long until he felt a tug on the line, and we watched the bobber go under.
3. He was the only one to go home with something other than bait!

1. The little girl cried as she stood looking up into the maple tree.
2. Between her tears, she managed to say, "My kitten is up in the tree and can't get down."
3. ______________________

1. Dad hung up the phone and turned to look at us.
2. ______________________
3. "This would be a good time to get out those old board games in the hall closet," he said.

Name: ____________________

Reading Skills: Sequencing

Directions: In each group below, one event in the sequence is missing. Write a sentence that makes sense in the sequence.

1. The traffic light turned red.
2. ______________________________

____
3. The police arrived to investigate.

1. ______________________________

____
2. She and her mother spent all morning going from store to store.
3. Megan was quite pleased with her new clothes.

1. The weatherman said that we could expect a heavy snowfall during the night.
2. When Dad got home from work, he told us the roads were getting very slippery.
3. ______________________________

____

1. Mom opened the kitchen drawer and reached in.
2. ______________________________

____
3. "Jody, please go get a bandage for me from the bathroom," she said.

Name: ____________________

Reading Skills: Sequencing

Directions: In each group below, one event in the sequence is missing. Write a sentence that makes sense in the sequence.

1. The clouds grew very dark and we could hear thunder.
2. All of a sudden, the wind started to blow very hard.
3. ____________________

1. The volleyball game was very boring at first.
2. ____________________
3. The home crowd cheered so loudly that I had to cover my ears.

1. ____________________
2. The boys gathered all the garden tools and put them in the wheelbarrow.
3. "Well, it was hard work, but we got it done, boys!" said Jim.

1. The teacher gave us our homework assignment early in the day.
2. Since the school assembly had to be cancelled, we had an extra study hall.
3. ____________________

1. Our cat has been acting very strange lately.
2. We heard unusual noises coming from the hall closet.
3. ____________________

Name: ______________________

Reading Skills: Jonny's Story

Directions: Read the following true story about a little boy. Pay careful attention to the details. As you read, think about the beginning, middle and end of the story.

Jonny got out of bed. It hurt for him to walk. He could hear his mother calling for him so he limped over to the top of the stairs.

"Jonny, hurry up. I have to get to work," his mom called from the kitchen. When 3 1/2-year-old Jonny didn't hurry down the stairs, his mother went to the door and called again. As she looked up, she noticed that he was moving very slowly. "I guess you will have to eat your breakfast at the sitter's house since we are running so late."

"Mom, my leg hurts," Jonny said. His mother bent down to take a look. Jonny's left ankle was slightly red and swollen.

"I'm sure it does hurt," his mother said as she lifted him up and sat him on the counter to get a closer look. "It feels warm, too. I should call the doctor and try to get an appointment for you today."

It was hard to leave him at the sitter's, but Jonny's mom knew she could call as soon as the doctor's office opened. She left him at the sitter's with an extra big hug and asked the sitter to call if Jonny got any worse.

The appointment was scheduled for later that afternoon. Jonny's mom picked him up from the sitter's and found that Jonny had slept most of the day. He also had a fever. "I'm glad you have an appointment for him at the doctor's," said the sitter.

Name: ______________________

Reading Skills: Jonny's Story

Jonny's mom sat in the busy waiting room as one patient after another was called in to see the doctor. The whole time she sat there, she held him. He slept the whole time. Usually he was a very busy little boy, so his mom knew he must not be feeling well.

"With his high fever and that swollen ankle, he must have picked up an infection," said the doctor. "This prescription for an antibiotic should have him feeling much better and running around in no time!"

It was quite the opposite, Jonny's family soon discovered. The next morning, Jonny's mom stayed home from work because he was worse, not better. By late afternoon, his fever rose to 105 degrees! "Better bring him into the emergency room," said the doctor.

Jonny was admitted to the hospital and had test after test. Many doctors, some of them specialists, were called in, but no one had an answer. One doctor did have a guess. The pediatrician wondered aloud, "Do you suppose it could be JRA (juvenile rheumatoid arthritis)?"

More tests were done at another hospital, and the pediatrician's diagnosis was confirmed—Jonny did have JRA. This "little boy" is now 29 years old and still has rheumatoid arthritis. He has had many operations and has to take medicine every day for the pain, but he is able to lead a happy, normal life.

Name: ____________________

Reading Skills: Sequencing

Directions: Reread the story, if necessary. Then choose an important event from the beginning, middle and end of the story, and write it below.

Beginning: ____________________

____

____

Middle: ____________________

____

____

End: ____________________

____

____

____

____

____

Directions: Number these story events in the order in which they happened.

________ Jonny's mom called the doctor to get an appointment since Jonny's ankle was red and swollen.

________ Jonny limped to the top of the stairs.

________ The pediatrician thought Jonny might have JRA.

________ The sitter told Jonny's mom that he had slept most of the day.

________ The doctor gave them a prescription for an antibiotic.

________ Jonny is now 29 years old.

________ Jonny told his mom, "My leg hurts."

Name: ____________________

Reading Skills: Recalling Details

Directions: Answer the questions below about "Jonny's Story."

1. How old was Jonny when his ankle began to bother him? ____________________
2. Why did Jonny's mom stay home from work the second day? ____________________

   ____

3. What do the letters JRA stand for? ____________________
4. When Jonny and his mom were waiting to see the doctor, how did Jonny's mom know he must not be feeling well? ____________________
5. Where did Jonny's mom take him when she picked him up at the sitter's house?

   ____

Directions: Write the letter of the definition beside the word it defines. If you need help, use a dictionary or check the context of the story.

a. strong medicine used to treat infections
b. found to be true
c. doctor that specializes in child care
d. not yet an adult
e. did not walk correctly

________ pediatrician

________ antibiotic

________ confirmed

________ limped

________ juvenile

Name: 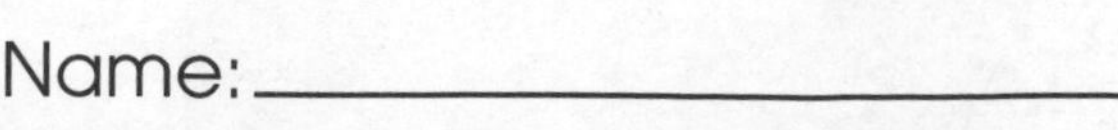

Reading Skills: Class Field Trip

Directions: Read this story about a class field trip. Pay careful attention to the details. As you read, think about the beginning, middle and end of the story.

Megan was very excited on her way to school. This was the day her fourth-grade class was going on its field trip to the town historical museum. As she looked out the bus window, she noticed that the bus was stopping at her friend Emily's house. She watched as Emily and her little sister climbed aboard the bus.

"I see you remembered your sack lunch," said Megan as her friend plopped down into the seat next to her.

"Remember? How could I forget?" said Emily breathlessly. "That's all we've talked about in class for the last two days."

The girls knew everyone was looking forward to the trip. Some children in the class were looking forward to the trip because they usually didn't get to ride a bus to school. Others in the class had been enjoying the study of their town's history and learning about what early life had been like for their ancestors. The girls laughed as they remembered what their classmate Paul had said, "I can't wait for the field trip—a day out of school!"

Soon they were at school and joined the rest of the fourth graders in homeroom. Obviously, by the chatter around them, their classmates were just as excited as they were.

Name: 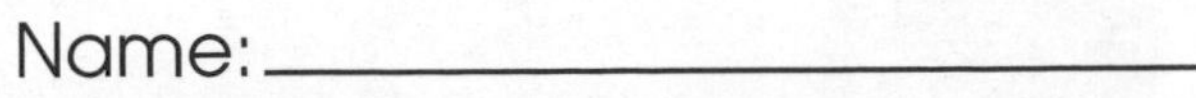

Reading Skills: Class Field Trip

"Take your seats, class," said the Miss Haynes. "No one gets on the bus for the trip until we take care of some business first. After I check attendance and all of you have your name tags, we can think about getting lined up. While I check attendance, Ms. Diehl and Mrs. Denes will collect your lunch sacks and put them in the cooler. Make sure your names are on your lunch sacks, please!"

All heads turned and looked at the back of the room as Paul let out a loud moan. "Oh, no! I left my lunch at home on the table by the door!"

Miss Haynes said, "Fortunately, the cafeteria will be able to put together a sack lunch for you." She wrote a note to the kitchen staff to explain the problem and sent a much happier Paul on his way down the hall. "Hurry, Paul, we load the bus for our trip in 10 minutes."

"Don't worry, Miss Haynes, I'll be there in time!" replied Paul as he hurried out the door.

True to his word, Paul returned, sack lunch in hand, with plenty of time to spare. Business was soon taken care of and the children and adults were on the bus, heading for their exciting day at the museum.

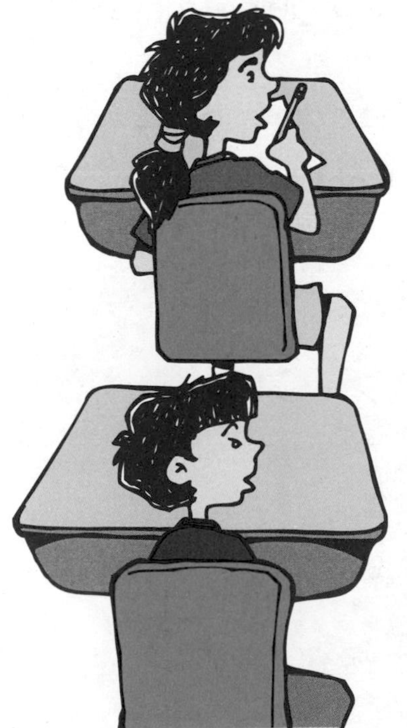

Name: ____________________

Reading Skills: Sequencing

Directions: Reread the story, if necessary. Then choose an important event from the beginning, middle and end of the story, and write it below.

Beginning: ____________________

____

Middle: ____________________

____

End: ____________________

____

Directions: Number these story events in the order in which they happened.

_______ Paul moaned, "Oh, no! I left my lunch on the table at home!"

_______ Megan watched as the bus stopped at Emily's house to pick up Emily and her little sister.

_______ Miss Haynes sent Paul to the cafeteria with a note explaining the problem.

_______ The teacher said they had some business to take care of before they could leave on the trip.

_______ Paul quickly returned with a sack lunch packed by the cafeteria helpers.

_______ Megan told Emily, "I see you remembered your sack lunch."

_______ The fourth graders finally loaded onto the bus for the field trip.

Name: ______________________

Reading Skills: Recalling Details

Directions: Answer the questions below about "Class Field Trip."

1. Who were the two adult helpers that would be going on the trip with Miss Haynes' class? ______________________

2. The students in Miss Haynes' class were excited about the field trip for different reasons. What were the three different reasons mentioned in the story?

   a. ______________________

   b. ______________________

   c. ______________________

3. What business did Miss Haynes need to take care of before the class could leave on its trip? ______________________

Directions: Write the letter of the definition beside the word it defines. If you need help, use a dictionary or check the context of the story.

a. sat down, not very gently
b. easy to understand; without doubt
c. family members that lived in the past, such as grandparents
d. in a favorable way

________ ancestors

________ fortunately

________ plopped

________ obviously

Name: 

Reading Skills: Sequencing

Directions: Read about how a tadpole becomes a frog. Then number the stages in order below.

Frogs and toads belong to a group of animals called amphibians (am-FIB-ee-ans). This means "living a double life." Frogs and toads live a "double life" because they live part of their lives in water and part on land. They are able to do this because their bodies change as they grow. This series of changes is called metamorphosis (met-a-MORE-fa-sis).

A mother frog lays her eggs in water and then leaves them on their own to grow. The eggs contain cells—the tiny "building blocks" of all living things—that multiply and grow. Soon the cells grow into a swimming tadpole. Tadpoles breathe through gills—small holes in their sides—like fish do. They spend all of their time in the water.

The tadpole changes as it grows. Back legs slowly form. Front legs begin inside the tadpole under the gill holes. They pop out when they are fully developed. At the same time, lungs, which a frog uses to breathe instead of gills, are almost ready to be used.

As the tadpole reaches the last days of its life in the water, its tail seems to disappear. When all of the tadpole's body parts are ready for life on land, it has become a frog.

________ The front legs pop out. The lungs are ready to use for breathing.

________ The cells in the egg multiply and grow.

________ The tadpole has become a frog.

________ Back legs slowly form.

________ Soon the cells grow into a swimming tadpole.

________ Front legs develop inside the tadpole.

________ The tadpole's tail seems to disappear.

________ A mother frog lays her eggs in water.

Name: ______________________

Reading Skills: Main Idea in Sentences

The **main idea** is the most important idea, or main point, in a sentence, paragraph or story.

Directions: Circle the main idea for each sentence.

1. Emily knew she would be late if she watched the end of the TV show.
   a. Emily likes watching TV.
   b. Emily is always running late.
   c. If Emily didn't leave, she would be late.

2. The dog was too strong and pulled Jason across the park on his leash.
   a. The dog is stronger than Jason.
   b. Jason is not very strong.
   c. Jason took the dog for a walk.

3. Jennifer took the book home so she could read it over and over.
   a. Jennifer loves to read.
   b. Jennifer loves the book.
   c. Jennifer is a good reader.

4. Jerome threw the baseball so hard it broke the window.
   a. Jerome throws baseballs very hard.
   b. Jerome was mad at the window.
   c. Jerome can't throw very straight.

5. Lori came home and decided to clean the kitchen for her parents.
   a. Lori is a very nice person.
   b. Lori did a favor for her parents.
   c. Lori likes to cook.

6. It was raining so hard that it was hard to see the road through the windshield.
   a. It always rains hard in April.
   b. The rain blurred our vision.
   c. It's hard to drive in the rain.

Name: ________________________

Reading Skills: Main Idea in Paragraphs

Directions: Read each paragraph below. Then circle the sentence that tells the main idea.

It looked as if our class field day would have to be cancelled due to the weather. We tried not to show our disappointment, but Mr. Wade knew that it was hard to keep our minds on the math lesson. We noticed that even he had been sneaking glances out the window. All morning the classroom had been buzzing with plans. Each team met to plan team strategies for winning the events. Then, it happened! Clouds began to cover the sky, and soon the thunder and lightning confirmed what we were afraid of—field day cancelled. Mr. Wade explained that we could still keep our same teams. We could put all of our plans into motion, but we would have to get busy and come up with some inside games and competitions. I guess the day would not be a total disaster!

a. Many storms occur in the late afternoon.

b. Our class field day had to be cancelled due to the weather.

c. Each team came up with its own strategies.

Allison and Emma had to work quietly and quickly to get Mom's birthday cake baked before she got home from work. Each of the girls had certain jobs to do—Allison set the oven temperature and got the cake pans prepared, while Emma got out all the ingredients. As they stirred and mixed, the two girls talked about the surprise party Dad had planned for Mom. Even Dad didn't know that the girls were baking this special cake. The cake was delicious. "It shows you what teamwork can do!" said the girls in unison.

a. Dad worked with the girls to bake the cake.

b. Mom's favorite frosting is chocolate cream.

c. Allison and Emma baked a birthday cake for Mom.

Name: ___________________

Reading Skills: Main Idea in Paragraphs

Directions: Read each paragraph below. Then circle the sentence that tells the main idea.

During the summer, Lori got a job at the city animal shelter. She loved petting the kittens and hearing them purr. She loved washing the dogs and watching them run around the yard. It was always fun and exciting to watch new animals come in, but it was even better watching animals get new homes with good families. When the city threatened to close the shelter due to money problems, Lori worked hard at a special car wash, bake sale and other fund-raisers to raise money. Luckily, they kept the shelter open! Lori said she would continue working even when school started, because she felt she was doing something worthwhile to help her community.

a. The animal shelter was almost closed by the city.

b. Lori loved working at the animal shelter.

c. Lori loved petting the animals.

Gary worked as a lifeguard last summer at the resort. One afternoon, a young girl and her mother came to the poolside to play. While the girl's mother went to get some iced tea, the little girl ran around the pool, playing with her new toys. Gary watched carefully and told the girl not to run, but she was too busy playing to pay attention. Just as Gary was climbing off the lifeguard stand to stop the girl from hurting herself, she slipped and fell into the deep end of the pool. Gary jumped in after her just in time. She didn't know how to swim. Just as Gary was lifting the girl from the water, her mother ran back to the pool. The girl was fine, but Gary warned her mother never to leave her daughter unattended by the pool, not even for a minute. The little girl was fine, and her mother was forever grateful for Gary's watchful eyes.

a. Young children should never be left unattended by the pool.

b. Being a lifeguard can be rewarding.

c. Gary saved a little girl from drowning last summer.

Name: ____________________

Reading Skills: Main Idea in Poetry

Directions: Read the verse from this poem written by Lord Tennyson, "The Charge of the Light Brigade." Then answer the questions below.

"Forward the Light Brigade!"

Was there a man dismayed?
Not though the soldier knew
    Someone had blundered.
Theirs not to make reply,
Theirs not to reason why,
Theirs but to do and die.
Into the valley of Death
    Rode the six hundred.

1. Circle the main idea:

   Soldiers in battle always fight in groups of 600.

   Soldiers in battle must follow orders without question.

2. What word in the verse means "made a mistake"? ____________________

3. What two things must a soldier not do?

   a. ____________________

   b. ____________________

4. What does Tennyson say is the responsibility of a soldier?

   ____

Name: ____________________

Reading Skills: Fact and Opinion

A **fact** is a statement that can be proven true. An **opinion** is a statement that tells how someone feels or what he/she thinks about something or someone.

Example:
Fact: Ms. Davis is the new principal at Hayes Elementary.
Opinion: Ms. Davis is the nicest principal we ever had.

Directions: Read each pair of sentences below. One is a fact; one is an opinion. Write **F** before the fact and **O** before the opinion.

_____ 1. Soccer is the best sport at our school.

_____ More students at our school play soccer than any other sport.

_____ 2. Grandmother Hall lives in Clarksburg.

_____ Grandmother Hall makes the best chocolate-chip cookies!

_____ 3. The county fair gate opens at 10:00 a.m.

_____ We're going to have a great time at the fair.

_____ 4. The drive along the river is very scenic.

_____ It is a 5-mile drive along the river.

_____ 5. Computers make our work much easier.

_____ We have four computers in our classroom.

_____ 6. *The Cinnamon Lake Mysteries* is a very good series.

_____ Our library has several copies of *The Cinnamon Lake Mysteries.*

_____ 7. Jerry falls asleep in class every day!

_____ Jerry is so tired, he can't stay awake.

_____ 8. That car is too old to make it across the country.

_____ That car was built in 1964.

Name: ____________________

Fact and Opinion

Directions: Write **F** before the facts and **O** before the opinions.

_____ 1. Our school football team has a winning season this year.

_____ 2. Mom's spaghetti is the best in the world!

_____ 3. Autumn is the nicest season of the year.

_____ 4. Mrs. Burns took her class on a field trip last Thursday.

_____ 5. The library always puts 30 books in our classroom book collection.

_____ 6. They should put only books about horses in the collection.

_____ 7. Our new art teacher is very strict.

_____ 8. Everyone should keep take-home papers in a folder so they don't have to look for them when it is time to go home.

_____ 9. The bus to the mall goes right by her house at 7:45 a.m.

_____ 10. Our new superintendent, Mr. Willeke, is very nice.

Name: ______________________

Fact and Opinion

Directions: Each fact sentence below has a "partner" opinion sentence in the box. Match "partners" by writing the correct sentences on the lines.

Maps can be very difficult to figure out.	Those brownies tasted awful!
The bridesmaids' dresses turned out beautiful!	Each child in here needs a computer.
You make the best cherry pie.	She is the best artist in the class.
If I can't go to the party, I will be really upset.	That car is so old, it looks like it will fall apart.

1. Paige helped her mother bake brownies last night.

____

2. Katherine made all the drawings for the book.

____

3. That cherry tree is full of cherries.

____

4. We have four computers in the classroom.

____

5. Mom made dresses for all of my bridesmaids.

____

6. If I can't go to the party, I won't be able to give her the present.

____

7. The car is old and rusty.

____

8. However he looked at it, he still couldn't figure out the map.

____

Name: ____________________

Review

Directions: Read the paragraph. Then circle the sentence that tells the main idea.

Justin and Mina did everything together. They rode their bikes to school together, ate their lunches together, did their homework together, and even spent their weekends together playing baseball and video games. Even though Justin and Mina sometimes argued about silly things, they still loved being together. Sometimes the arguments were even fun, because then they got to make up! People often thought they were brother and sister because they sounded alike and even looked alike! Justin and Mina promised they would be friends forever.

a. Justin and Mina did everything together.

b. Justin and Mina like riding bikes.

c. Justin and Mina like to argue.

Directions: Write **F** before the facts and **O** before the opinions.

_____ 1. Justin loved to ride his bike.

_____ 2. Mina promised they would always be friends.

_____ 3. Justin and Mina should never argue.

_____ 4. Justin's dog needed to be washed.

_____ 5. That car is only big enough for three people!

_____ 6. The laundry basket is in the corner of the basement.

_____ 7. That laundry needs to be done today.

_____ 8. Brownies are my favorite snack.

_____ 9. She made chocolate cake for Mom's birthday.

_____ 10. I came all the way from Texas to see you.

Name: ______________________

Reading Comprehension: Your Five Senses

Your senses are very important to you. You depend on them every day. They tell you where you are and what is going on around you. Your senses are sight, hearing, touch, smell and taste.

Try to imagine for a minute that you were suddenly unable to use your senses. Imagine, for instance, that you are in a cave and your only source of light is a candle. Without warning, a gust of wind blows out the flame.

Your senses are always at work. Your eyes let you read this book. Your nose brings the scent of dinner cooking. Your hand feels the softness as you stroke a puppy. Your ears tell you that a storm is approaching.

Your senses also help keep you from harm. They warn you if you touch something that will burn you. They keep you from looking at a light that is too bright, and they tell you if a car is coming up behind you. Each of your senses collects information and sends it as a message to your brain. The brain is like the control center for your body. It sorts out the messages sent by your senses and acts on them.

Directions: Answer these questions about the five senses.

1. Circle the main idea:

   Your senses keep you from harm.

   Your senses are important to you in many ways.

2. Name the five senses.

   a. ______________________

   b. ______________________

   c. ______________________

   d. ______________________

   e. ______________________

3. Which part of your body acts as the "control center"?

   ____

Name: ____________________

Reading Comprehension: Touch

Unlike the other senses, which are located only in your head, your sense of touch is all over your body. Throughout your life, you receive an endless flow of information about the world and yourself from your sense of touch. It tells you if something is hot or cold, hard or soft. It sends messages of pain, such as a headache or sore throat, if there is a problem.

There are thousands of tiny sensors all over your body. They are all linked together. These sensors are also linked to your spinal cord and your brain to make up your central nervous system. Through this system, the various parts of your body can send messages to your brain. It is then the brain's job to decide what it is you are actually feeling. All this happens in just a split second.

Not all parts of your body have the same amount of feeling. Areas that have the most nerves, or sensors, have the greatest amount of feeling. For instance, the tips of your fingers have more feeling than parts of your arm.

Some sensors get used to the feeling of an object after a period of time. When you first put your shirt on in the morning, you can feel its pressure on your skin. However, some of the sensors stop responding during the day.

One feeling you cannot get used to is the feeling of pain. Pain is an important message, because it tells your brain that something harmful is happening to you. Your brain reacts by doing something right away to protect you.

Directions: Answer these questions about the sense of touch.

1. Circle the main idea:

   The sense of touch is all over your body.

   You cannot get used to the sense of pain.

2. The nerves, spinal cord and brain are linked together to make the ____________________

   ____.

3. One feeling you can never get used to is ____________________.

4. All parts of your body have the same amount of feeling. True False

5. It is the brain's job to receive messages from the sensors on your body and decide what you are actually feeling. True False

Name: ____________________

Reading Comprehension: Smell

Your nose is your sense organ for smelling. Smells are mixed into the air around you. They enter your nose when you breathe.

In the upper part of your nose, there are special smell sensors. They pick up smells and send messages to your brain. The brain then decides what it is you are smelling.

Smelling can be a pleasant sense. Sometimes smells can remind you of a person or place. For instance, have you ever smelled a particular scent and then suddenly thought about your grandmother's house? Smell also can make you feel hungry. In fact, your sense of smell is linked very closely to your sense of taste. Without your sense of smell, you would not taste food as strongly.

Smelling also can be quite unpleasant. But this, too, is important. By smelling food you can tell if it is spoiled and not fit to eat. Your sense of smell also can sometimes warn you of danger, such as a fire.

The sense of smell tires out more quickly than your other senses. This is why you get used to some everyday smells and no longer notice them after a while.

Directions: Answer these questions about the sense of smell.

1. Smells are mixed in ____________________.

2. The sense of smell is linked closely to the sense of ____________________.

3. Give an example of why smelling bad smells can be important to you.

____

____

Name: 

Reading Comprehension: Taste

The senses of taste and smell work very closely together. If you can't smell your food, it is difficult to recognize the taste. You may have noticed this when you've had a bad cold with a stuffed-up nose.

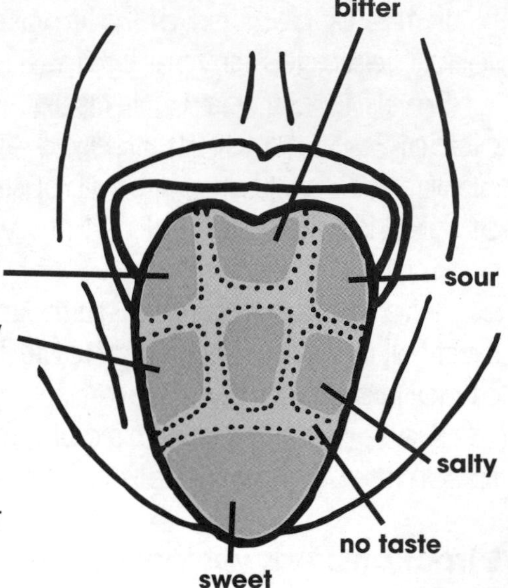

Tasting is the work of your tongue. All over your tongue are tiny taste sensors called taste buds. If you look at your tongue in a mirror, you can see small groups of taste buds. They are what give your tongue its rough appearance. Each taste bud has a small opening in it. Tiny pieces of food and drink enter this opening. There taste sensors gather information about the taste and send messages to your brain. Your brain decides what the taste is.

Taste buds located in different areas of your tongue recognize different tastes. There are only four tastes your tongue can recognize: sweet, sour, bitter and salty. All other flavors are a mixture of taste and smell.

Directions: Answer these questions about the sense of taste.

1. It is difficult to taste your food if you can't ______________________________.

2. The tiny taste sensors on your tongue are called ______________________________.

3. The four tastes that your tongue can recognize are ______________________________

____.

4. All other flavors are a mixture of ______________________________.

Name: ______________________

Reading Comprehension: Sight

You can see this page because of light. Without light, there would be no sight. In a dark room, you might see only a a few large shapes. If it is pitch black, you can't see anything at all.

Light reflects or bounces off things and then travels to your eyes. The light enters your eye through the pupil. The pupil is the black circle in the middle of your eye. It gets bigger in low light to let in as much light as possible. In bright light, it shrinks so that too much light doesn't get in.

Light enters through the pupil and then passes through the lens. The lens bends the light so that it falls on the back of your eye on the retina. The retina has millions of tiny cells that are very sensitive to light. When an image is formed in the eye, it is upside down. This image is sent to your brain. The brain receives the message and turns the picture right side up again.

Some people are far-sighted. This means they can clearly see things that are far away, but things close by may be blurred. People who are near-sighted can clearly see things better if they are close by. Glasses or contact lenses can help correct these problems.

Some people can see only a little bit or perhaps not at all. This is called being blind. Blind people rely on their sense of touch to learn more about the world. They can even use their sense of touch to read. Some blind people read with a special printing system called Braille. The system is named for the man who invented it. Braille has small raised dots instead of letters on a page.

Directions: Answer these questions about the sense of sight.

1. Without ______________________, there would be no sight.
2. Reflect means ______________________.
3. The part of the eye that controls the amount of light entering your eye by getting bigger and smaller is called the ______________________.
4. To correct near-sightedness or far-sightedness, you can wear ______________________ ______________________.
5. What is the name of the special printing system for blind people? ______________________

Name: ____________________

Reading Comprehension: Hearing

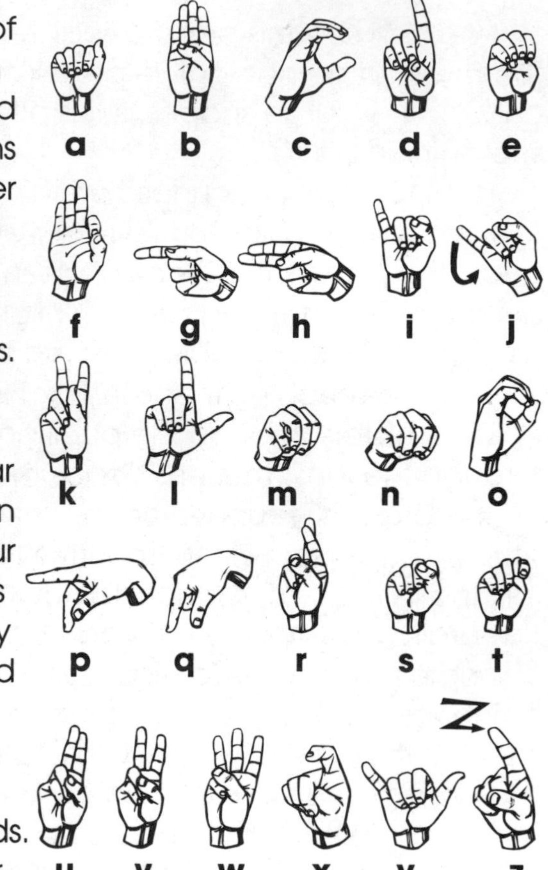

Every sound you hear is made by the movement of air. These movements, called vibrations, spread out in waves. Your outer ear collects these "sound waves" and sends them down a tube to the inner ear. The vibrations hit the eardrum, a flap of skin stretched across the inner end of the tube. As the eardrum vibrates, a tiny bone called the hammer moves back and forth. This helps the vibrations move to three small bones and then to the cochlea, where they are changed to nerve impulses. The impulses travel to the brain where they are recognized as sounds.

Some people have trouble hearing or cannot hear at all. This is called being deaf. Some deaf people can understand what you are saying by watching how your lips move. They use their eyes as their ears. Sometimes a hearing aid can help improve hearing. It is like a tiny radio that fits into the ear. Sounds enter the hearing aid and are made much louder.

Deaf people also have difficulty learning to speak because they cannot hear how to say words. Many deaf people "talk" by making pictures with their hands. This kind of talking is called sign language. Every letter of the alphabet has a sign. These signs are shown above.

Directions: Answer these questions about the sense of hearing.

1. Sound is made by movements of the air called ____________________.

2. The flap of skin stretched over the inner end of the tube inside your ear is called

   the ____________________.

3. People who cannot hear are said to be ____________________.

4. The language of making pictures with your hands is called ____________________.

5. Read this word in sign language.

   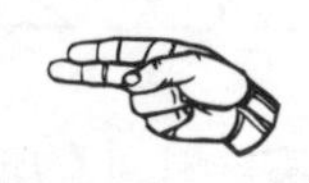   

   It says ____________________.

Name: ______________________

Reading Comprehension: The Five Senses

Directions: Before each sentence, write the sense—hearing, sight, smell, taste or touch—that is being used. The first one is done for you.

hearing 1. The rooster crows outside my window early each morning.

________ 2. After playing in the snow, our fingers and toes were freezing.

________ 3. I could hear sirens in the distance.

________ 4. I think this tree is taller than that one.

________ 5. The delicious salad was filled with fresh, juicy fruits.

________ 6. The odor of the bread baking in the oven was wonderful.

________ 7. There was a rainbow in the sky today.

________ 8. The kitten was soft and fluffy.

________ 9. Her perfume filled the air when she walked by.

________ 10. An airplane wrote a message in the sky.

________ 11. The chocolate cake was yummy.

________ 12. The steamboat whistle frightened the baby.

________ 13. The sour lemon made my lips pucker.

________ 14. Her gum-popping got on my nerves.

Name: ____________________

Reading Comprehension: The Five Senses

Directions: Each word in the word box makes you think of hearing, sight, smell, taste or touch. Write each word under the sense that is used. One is done for you.

music	rainbow	talking	hot	sour
honking	moldy	butterfly	green	book
crying	~~silky~~	sweet	smoky	bitter
salty	skunk	cold	smooth	stinky

Touch

silky

____

____

____

Sight

____

____

____

____

Taste

____

____

____

____

Smell

____

____

____

____

Hearing

____

____

____

____

Name: ____________________

Reading Comprehension: Helen Keller

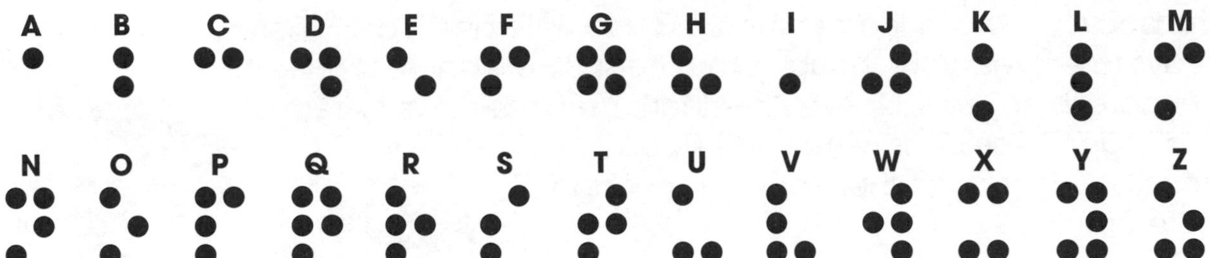

The story of Helen Keller has given courage and hope to many people. Helen had many problems, but she used her life to do great things.

When Helen Keller was a child, she often behaved in a wild way. She was very bright and strong, but she could not tell people what she was thinking or feeling. And she didn't know how others thought or felt. Helen was blind and deaf.

Helen was born with normal hearing and sight, but this changed when she was 1 year old. She had a serious illness with a very high fever. After that, Helen was never able to see or hear again.

As a child, Helen was angry and lonely. But when she was 6 years old, her parents got a teacher for her. They brought a young woman named Anne Sullivan to stay at their house and help Helen. After much hard work, Helen began to learn sign language. Anne taught Helen many important things, such as how to behave like other children. Because Helen was so smart, she learned things very quickly. She learned how to read Braille. By the time she was 8 years old, she was becoming very famous. People were amazed at what she could do.

Helen continued to learn. She even learned how to speak. When she was 20 years old, she went to college. Helen did so well in college that a magazine paid her to write the story of her life. After college, she earned money by writing and giving speeches. She traveled all around the world. She worked to get special schools and libraries for the blind and deaf. She wrote many books, including one about her teacher, Anne Sullivan.

Here is how "Helen" is written in Braille: 

Directions: Answer these questions about Helen Keller.

1. What caused Helen to be blind and deaf? ____________________

____

2. What happy thing happened when Helen was 6 years old? ____________________

____

3. What was her teacher's name? ____________________

Name: 

Review

In this book, you have learned new ways to write and "talk." There are many other ways to express your thoughts to others. Here is another one.

For hundreds of years, Native Americans used their own system of sign language. These signs were understood by all tribes, even though their spoken languages were different.

The Plains tribes helped to develop and spread sign language. The Plains tribes liked to wander. They never camped in any one place for long. They used sign language so they could talk with other Native Americans wherever they went.

The first white adventurers and trappers in America also learned Native American sign language. They wanted to understand and be understood by the Native Americans.

Many Native Americans today still use this ancient form of talking. It is no longer necessary, but it is an important link to their past.

Directions: Answer these questions about sign language.

1. Circle the main idea:

   Native Americans used a kind of sign language.

   There are many ways to express your thoughts to others.

2. Every tribe had its own sign language. True False

3. The Plains tribes did not use sign language. True False

4. Many Native Americans today still use this sign language. True False

5. Sign language is still necessary among Native Americans. True False

Name: ____________________

Reading Comprehension: Mermaids

One of the most popular fantasy characters is the mermaid. Many different countries have stories about these lovely creatures, which are half woman and half fish. In these fables, the mermaid is always beautiful—except perhaps for her greenish skin and webbed fingers!

There are some stories about mermen, too. They are said to have fine torsos with big, strong muscles in their chests and arms. But they have the most ugly faces—eyes like a pig, red noses, green teeth and seaweed hair!

A famous fable told in Ireland tells about a mermaid who was said to have been seen nearly 1,400 years ago. The story says that she could be heard singing beneath the waters for many years. One day, some men rowed out and caught her with a net. They were surprised to learn that she had once been a little human girl. Her family had died in a flood. But she survived beneath the waves and gradually changed into a mermaid.

Directions: Answer these questions about story.

1. Which definition is correct for **fantasy**?

   ☐ from the imagination and not real ☐ real ☐ living in the sea

2. Which definition is correct for **fable**?

   ☐ a true story ☐ a made-up story ☐ a story about fish

3. Which definition is correct for **torso**?

   ☐ the head ☐ the upper body but not the head ☐ the lower body

4. Which definition is correct for **survived**?

   ☐ swam ☐ died ☐ continued to live

Name: ____________________

Reading Comprehension: Paul Bunyan

There is a certain kind of fable called a "tall tale." In these stories, each storyteller tries to "top" the other. The stories get more and more unbelievable. A popular hero of American tall tales is Paul Bunyan—a giant of a man. Here are some of the stories that have been told about him.

Even as a baby, Paul was very big. One night, he rolled over in his sleep and knocked down a mile of trees. Of course, Paul's father wanted to find some way to keep Paul from getting hurt in his sleep and to keep him from knocking down all the forests. So he cut down some tall trees and made a boat for Paul to use as a cradle. He tied a long rope to the boat and let it drift out a little way into the sea to rock Paul to sleep.

One night, Paul had trouble sleeping. He kept turning over in his bed. Each time he turned, the cradle rocked. And each time the cradle rocked, it sent up waves as big as buildings. The waves got bigger and bigger until the people on the land were afraid they would all be drowned. They told Paul's parents that Paul was a danger to the whole state! So Paul and his parents had to move away.

After that, Paul didn't get into much trouble when he was growing up. His father taught him some very important lessons, such as, "If there are any towns or farms in your way, be sure to step around them!"

Directions: Answer these questions about Paul Bunyan.

1. What kind of fable is the story of Paul Bunyan? ____________________

2. What did Paul's father make for Paul to use as a cradle? ____________________

3. What happened when Paul rolled over in his cradle? ____________________

____

4. What did Paul's father tell Paul to do to towns and farms that were in his way?

____

Name: ____________________

Reading Comprehension: Paul Bunyan

When Paul Bunyan grew up, he was taller than other men—by about 50 feet or so! Because of his size, he could do almost anything. One of the things he did best was to cut down trees and turn them into lumber. With only four strokes of his axe, he could cut off all the branches and bark. After he turned all the trees for miles into these tall square posts, he tied a long rope to an axe head. Then he yelled, "T-I-M-B-E-R-R-R!" and swung the rope around in a huge circle. With every swing, 100 trees fell to the ground.

One cold winter day, Paul found a huge blue ox stuck in the snow. It was nearly frozen. Although it was only a baby, even Paul could hardly lift it. Paul took the ox home and cared for it. He named it Babe, and they became best friends. Babe was a big help to Paul when he was cutting down trees.

When Babe was full grown, it was hard to tell how big he was. There were no scales big enough to weigh him. Paul once measured the distance between Babe's eyes. It was the length of 42 axe handles!

Once Paul and Babe were working with other men to cut lumber. The job was very hard because the road was so long and winding. It was said that the road was so crooked that men starting home for camp would meet themselves coming back! Well, Paul hitched Babe to the end of that crooked road. Babe pulled and pulled. He pulled so hard that his eyes nearly turned pink. There was a loud snap. The first curve came out of the road and Babe pulled harder. Finally the whole road started to move. Babe pulled it completely straight!

Directions: Answer these questions about Paul Bunyan and Babe.

1. What was Paul Bunyan particularly good at doing? ____________________
2. What did Paul find in the snow? ____________________
3. How big was the distance between Babe's eyes? ____________________
4. What did Babe do to the crooked road? ____________________

Name: ____________________

Reading Comprehension: Hummingbirds

Hummingbirds are very small birds. This tiny bird is quite an acrobat. Only a few birds, such as kingfishers and sunbirds, can hover, which means to stay in one place in the air. But no other bird can match the flying skills of the hummingbird. The hummingbird can hover, fly backward and fly upside down!

Hummingbirds got their name because their wings move very quickly when they fly. This causes a humming sound. Their wings move so fast that you can't see them at all. This takes a lot of energy. These little birds must have food about every 20 minutes to have enough strength to fly. Their favorite foods are insects and nectar. Nectar is the sweet water deep inside a flower. Hummingbirds use their long, thin bills to drink from flowers. When a hummingbird sips nectar, it hovers in front of a flower. It never touches the flower with its wings or feet.

Besides being the best at flying, the hummingbird is also one of the prettiest birds. Of all the birds in the world, the hummingbird's colors are among the brightest. Some are bright green with red and white markings. Some are purple. One kind of hummingbird can change its color from reddish-brown to purple to red!

The hummingbird's nest is special, too. It looks like a tiny cup. The inside of the nest is very soft. This is because one of the things the mother bird uses to build the nest is the silk from a spider's web.

Directions: Answer these questions about hummingbirds.

1. How did hummingbirds get their name? ____________________

   ____

2. What does **hover** mean? ____________________

3. How often do hummingbirds need to eat? ____________________

4. Name two things that hummingbirds eat. ____________________

5. What is one of the things a mother hummingbird uses to build her nest?

   ____

Name: ____________________

Reading Comprehension: Bats

Bats are the only mammals that can fly. They have wings made of thin skin stretched between long fingers. Bats can fly amazing distances. Some small bats have been known to fly more than 25 miles in one night.

Most bats eat insects or fruit. But some eat only fish, others only blood and still others the nectar and pollen of flowers that bloom at night. Bats are active only at night. They sleep during the day in caves or other dark places. At rest, they always hang with their heads down.

You may have heard the expression "blind as a bat." But bats are not blind. They don't, however, use their eyes to guide their flight or to find the insects they eat. A bat makes a high-pitched squeak, then waits for the echo to return to it. This echo tells it how far away an object is. This is often called the bat's sonar system. Using this system, a bat can fly through a dark cave without bumping into anything. Hundreds of bats can fly about in the dark without ever running into each other. They do not get confused by the squeaks of the other bats. They always recognize their own echoes.

Directions: Answer these questions about bats.

1. Bats are the only mammals that
   - ☐ eat insects. ☐ fly. ☐ live in caves.
2. Most bats eat
   - ☐ plants. ☐ other animals. ☐ fruits and insects.
3. Bats always sleep
   - ☐ with their heads down. ☐ lying down. ☐ during the night.
4. Bats are blind. True False
5. Bats use a built-in sonar system to guide them. True False
6. Bats are confused by the squeaks of other bats. True False

Name: ____________________

Reading Comprehension: Echoes

An echo is the repeating of a sound when it is reflected off a surface. For example, if you shout at a solid stone wall, your words often come back to you. This is your echo.

All sounds are made up of vibrations—very quick movements of the air. These vibrations move out in "sound waves." When a sound wave hits a hard, smooth surface, it is bent back. A rough surface breaks up the sound waves. In a valley with mountains all around, a may be echoed many times.

To experiment with echoes, stand at least 60 feet from the wall you will send the sound against. If you are any closer, the echo comes back too quickly. You would not be able to hear it as a separate sound because it would be mixed up with the original sound.

Directions: Answer these questions about echoes.

1. An echo occurs when sound waves are reflected off a surface. True False
2. Sounds are caused by vibrations of the air. True False
3. When sound hits a rough surface, it is bent back. True False
4. Sounds do not echo very well in a valley. True False
5. You must stand very close to a wall if you want to hear your echo. True False
6. What happens when a sound wave hits a hard, smooth surface?

   ____

7. How far away must you stand from a wall if you want to experiment with echoes?

   ____

8. Which word in the story means to try something as a test? ____________________
9. What are vibrations? ____

Name: ______________________

Reading Comprehension: Chameleons

Chameleons (ka-MEAL-yens) are the strangest of all lizards. They can change their colors among greens, browns, reds, yellows, white and black. This helps them hide. They can become the color of whatever they are standing next to.

Chameleons range in size from 1 1/2 inches to 2 feet. They have very long tongues and long tails that can grab onto things. As lizards, chameleons are members of the reptile family. Many reptiles, such as the snake, can move very fast. But chameleons move very, very slowly. They move one leg at a time and creep along as though they are afraid they will fall down.

All reptiles can move their eyes independently. That means they can look in different directions with each eye. This is very easy to see on the chameleon. The chameleon's eye is almost completely covered by the eyelid, with only a tiny hole in the middle when their eyes are open. The hole moves as the eye moves. You might see a chameleon with one eye pointing up and the other one pointing down.

A chameleon's tongue is longer than its head and body put together. It has a large, sticky spot on the end. When a chameleon sees an insect, he shoots his tongue out, catches it and then snaps his tongue back into his mouth and swallows the insect.

Directions: Answer these questions about chameleons.

1. A chameleon can change its ______________________________.

2. Chameleons belong to the family of ______________________________.

3. As with all reptiles, the chameleon can move its eyes ______________________________.

4. A chameleon's tongue is longer than

   ☐ its head. ☐ its body. ☐ its head and body put together.

5. A chameleon eats

   ☐ insects. ☐ fruit. ☐ nectar.

Name: 

Review: Venn Diagram

Directions: A **Venn diagram** is used to chart information that shows similarities and differences between two things. The Venn diagram below compares a mermaid (see page 73) and Paul Bunyan (see pages 74 and 75).

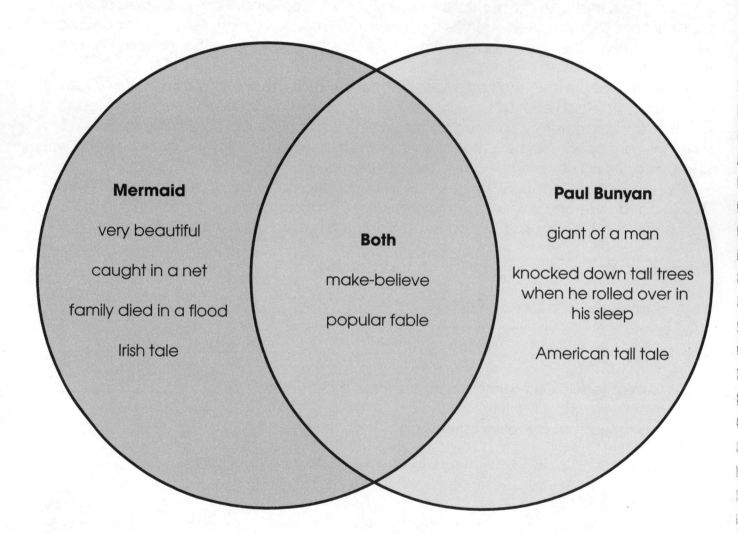

Mermaid

very beautiful

caught in a net

family died in a flood

Irish tale

Both

make-believe

popular fable

Paul Bunyan

giant of a man

knocked down tall trees when he rolled over in his sleep

American tall tale

Name:

Review: Venn Diagram

Directions: Make a Venn diagram comparing hummingbirds (see page 76) and bats (see page 77). Refer to the sample diagram on page 80 to help you. Write at least three characteristics for each section of the diagram.

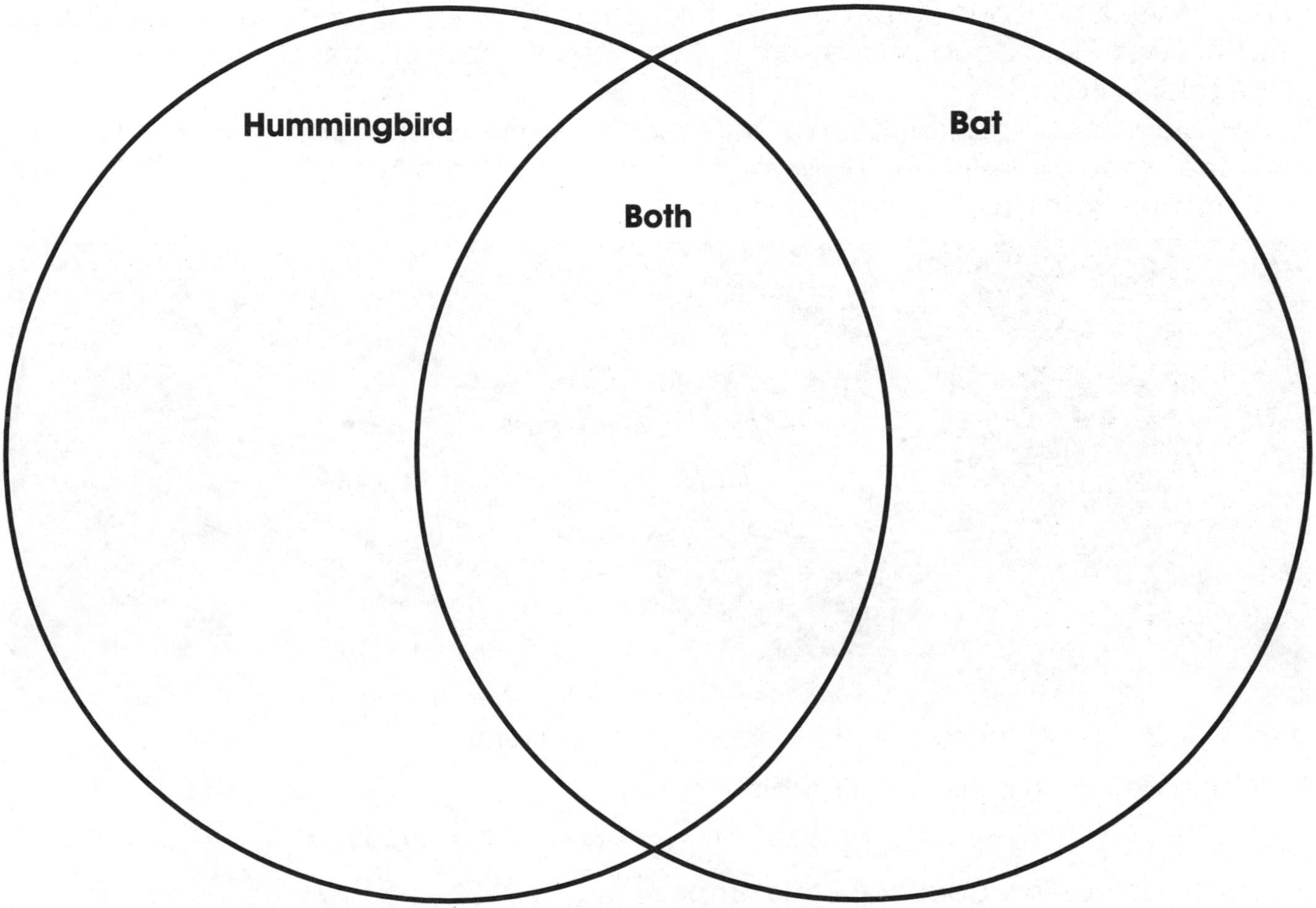

Hummingbird

Both

Bat

Name: ____________________

Reading Comprehension: The Solar System

You live on a planet—the planet Earth. It is one of nine planets that follows an orbit around the Sun. The other eight planets are Mercury, Venus, Mars, Jupiter, Saturn, Uranus, Neptune and Pluto. These nine planets are part of the solar system. The word **sol**, the ootbase word for **solar**, means sun. The Sun is at the center of the solar system and is very important. So, you could call the solar system the "Sun System."

You can see some of the planets by looking at the sky on a clear night. Mercury, Venus, Mars, Jupiter and Saturn look like bright stars. You need a telescope to see Uranus, Neptune and Pluto because they are not very bright. These planets are the most distant in the solar system.

The Moon is also part of the solar system. Just as Earth circles around the Sun in an orbit, the Moon circles Earth. This is why it is often called Earth's satellite. Most of the other planets have satellites, too. Jupiter has 16 moons! You need a telescope to see them.

Directions: Answer these questions about the solar system.

1. Which definition is correct for **orbit**?

   ☐ planet ☐ path ☐ moon

2. Which definition is correct for **telescope**?

   ☐ an instrument that makes distant objects seem closer and larger

   ☐ a flashlight

   ☐ an instrument to measure the size of planets

3. Which definition is correct for **satellite**?

   ☐ a small heavenly body in an orbit around a bigger one

   ☐ a path

   ☐ a solar system

Reading Comprehension: Planet Facts

It takes Earth 365 days—one year—to complete one orbit around the Sun. Mercury, the planet closest to the Sun, takes only 88 days to orbit the Sun. But Pluto takes about 248 years!

Because they are the farthest from the Sun, Neptune and Pluto are the coldest planets. Their temperatures are about 370 degrees below zero! Mercury and Venus are the hottest planets. The temperature can reach 620 degrees on Mercury and 882 degrees on Venus. Plants and animals cannot live on these planets because they would either freeze or burn up. In fact, scientists believe that Earth is the only planet in our solar system where plants, animals and people can live. This is why Earth is called the "living planet."

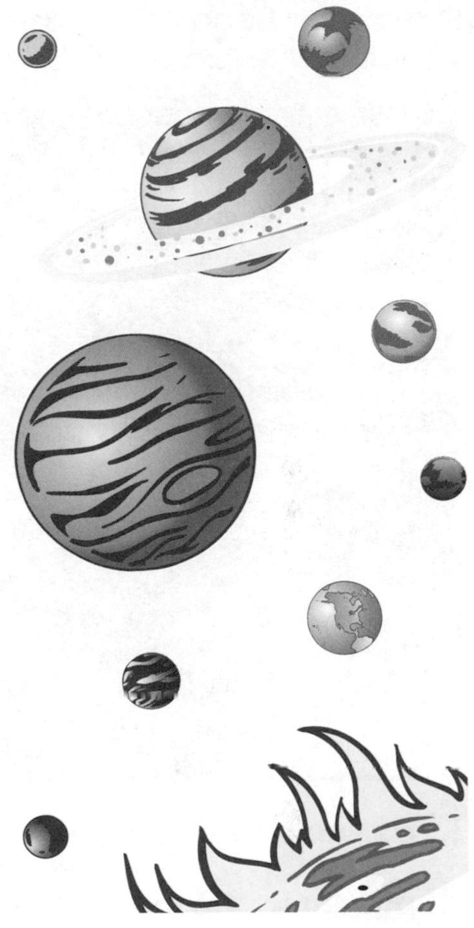

Earth is a middle-sized planet. Four of the planets are smaller than Earth. They are Mercury, Venus, Mars and Pluto. Jupiter, Saturn, Uranus and Neptune are all larger than Earth. Jupiter is the biggest planet. It is more than 1,000 times bigger than Earth. Pluto is the smallest planet. Earth is about four times bigger than Pluto.

The Sun is really a star. Stars are balls of hot, glowing gas. The Sun looks so much bigger than the other stars because it is so much closer. It is only 93 million miles away from Earth. The next closest star is 25 trillion miles away!

Directions: Answer these questions about the planets.

1. How many days does it take Earth to orbit the Sun? ______________________

2. Which are the two coldest planets? ______________________

3. Which are the two hottest planets? ______________________

4. What is Earth sometimes called? ______________________

5. Which planets are bigger than Earth? ______________________

____

6. What is a star? ______________________

Name: ______________________

Reading Comprehension: Planet Facts

Directions: Read about the planets. Then unscramble the name of each planet and write it on the line.

1. **peNnute** takes 165 years to complete its path, or orbit, around the Sun. ____________
2. **piteJur** has 16 moons orbiting around it. ____________
3. **oPult** is the coldest planet—400 degrees below zero! ____________
4. **sarM** is nicknamed the "red planet." ____________
5. **aruntS** is one of the most beautiful planets to look at through a telescope because of the many rings that surround it. ____________
6. **cryMure** is the planet closest to the Sun. ____________
7. **rathE** is sometimes called the "living planet." ____________
8. Until recent discoveries, **seVun** was thought of as the "mystery planet" because it is covered by thick clouds. ____________
9. **rUsanu** rotates lying on its side. ____________

Name: ____________________

Reading Comprehension: Mars and Earth

Earth is the only planet that scientists are certain has life. What does Earth have that the other planets don't? For one thing, Earth is just the right temperature. As the third planet from the sun, Earth seems to be just the right distance away. The planets closer to the Sun are so hot that their surfaces bake. The farthest planets are frozen balls.

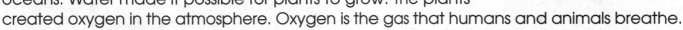

When Earth developed—which scientists believe may have happened about 4 billion years ago—many gases covered the planet. These gases caused Earth to be hot. But the temperature was just right for thick clouds to form. It rained very hard for a very long time. This gave Earth its oceans. Water made it possible for plants to grow. The plants created oxygen in the atmosphere. Oxygen is the gas that humans and animals breathe.

Only one other planet in the solar system seems to be anything like Earth. That planet is Mars. Mars is smaller than Earth, and it is quite a bit cooler. But it is not too cold for humans. On some days, the temperatures are as cold as a winter day in the northern United States. If you wore a special space suit, you could walk around on Mars. You would have to bring your own air to breathe, because the air on Mars is too thin.

Mars has the largest volcano in the solar system. It is 16 miles high. The highest volcano on Earth is 5 miles high. The most unexpected sights on Mars are dried-up riverbeds. Scientists believe that Mars was once much wetter. Does this mean there could have been living things on Mars? Scientists are not sure, but there has been no sign so far.

Directions: Answer these questions about Mars and Earth.

1. Name three things Earth has that makes life possible.

   a. ____________ b. ____________ c. ____________

2. According to scientists, how long ago did Earth develop? ____________

   ____

3. What planet is most like Earth? ____________

4. Mars has the biggest volcano in the solar system. How tall is it? ____________

5. Why can't you breathe on Mars? ____________

Name: 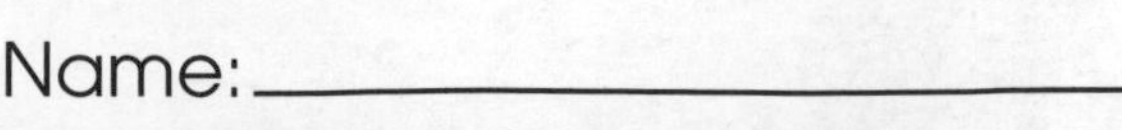

Reading Comprehension: The Moon

Earth has a partner in its trip around the Sun. It is the Moon. The Moon is Earth's satellite. It moves around Earth very quickly. It takes the Moon 28 days to go around Earth one time.

While they are partners in the solar system, the Earth and the Moon are very different. Earth is filled with life. It is a very colorful planet. The Moon is gray and lifeless. Nothing can live on the Moon.

There is no air on the Moon. Astronauts must wear special space suits when they walk on the Moon so they can breathe. The moon also has no water. There is no weather, so the sky above the Moon always looks black.

You would not weigh as much on the Moon as you do on Earth. If you weigh 100 pounds, you would weigh only 16 pounds on the Moon. It is very different to walk on the Moon, too. You would bounce and float!

Directions: Answer these questions about the Moon.

1. What is Earth's partner in the solar system? ____________________
2. How long does it take the Moon to go around Earth? ____________________
3. There is no life on the Moon. True False
4. There is lots of water on the Moon. True False
5. You would weigh more on the Moon than you do on Earth. True False

Name: ____________________

Reading Comprehension: Constellations

Constellations are pictures in the sky. The pictures are made of stars. There are 88 constellations in all. Some pictures are of animals from ancient Greek stories, such as horses that fly. There are also brave heroes and terrible monsters. The constellations are hard to find at first, but with practice, you can locate them.

The most famous star picture is called Ursa Major. This means "the Great Bear." There are many stars in this picture, but the seven stars that make up the body are very bright and easy to see. They look like a giant pan. You may have heard of this picture by its more common name—the Big Dipper. There is another constellation called Ursa Minor. It also is shaped like a pan, and is called the Little Dipper.

There is a group of 12 constellations called the Zodiac. They are lined up one after another all around the sky. Each month, a different member of the Zodiac rises in the east. Each day, more of it becomes visible. After 1 year, the entire picture has been overhead. Most of the pictures of the Zodiac are animals, including Taurus the bull and Scorpius the scorpion. The Scorpius is the biggest constellation in the Zodiac. There are pictures of people, too, such as Sagittarius, the archer, with his big bow and arrow.

Sagittarius 

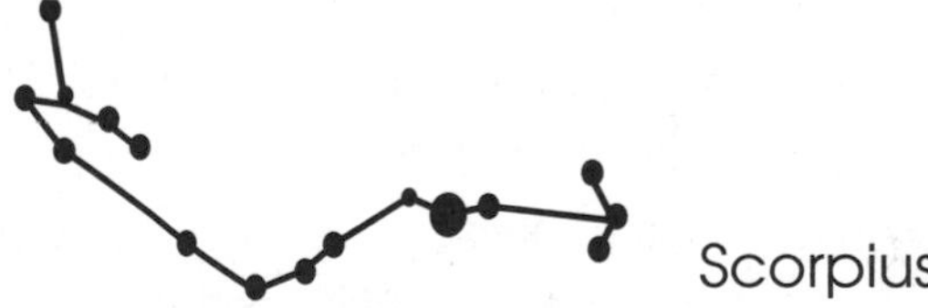 Scorpius

Directions: Answer these questions about constellations.

1. What is a constellation? ____________________
2. How many constellations are there? ____________________
3. What is the more common name for Ursa Major? ____________________
4. What is the name for the group of 12 constellations lined up around the sky?

   ____
5. What is the biggest constellation in the Zodiac? ____________________

Name: ____________________

Reading Comprehension: Telescopes

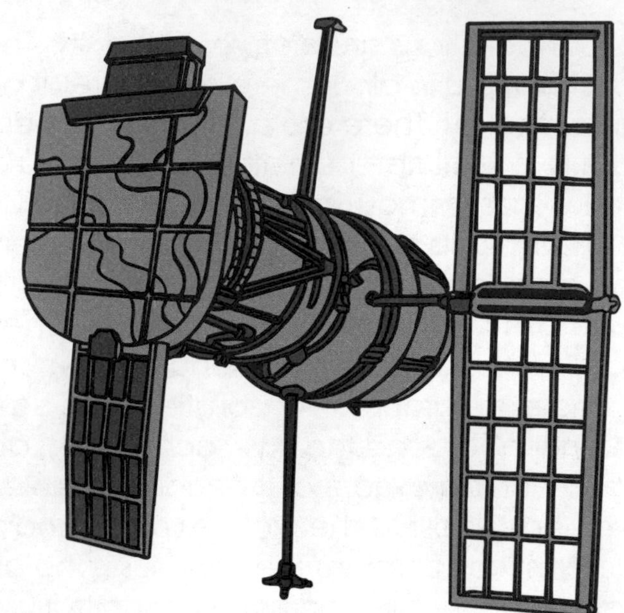

A telescope is an instrument that makes distant objects, such as the stars and planets, seem closer and bigger. This allows us to get a better look at them and scientists to learn more about them. In 1990, a very special telescope was launched into the sky aboard the space shuttle *Discovery*. The Hubble Space Telescope (HST), which is named for the man who invented it, cost almost 2 billion dollars to make.

HST is a powerful eye in the sky that may help answer questions scientists have asked for a long time: How did the universe begin? How will it end? Is there other life in the universe?

Scientists need big telescopes to explore the universe. On Earth, there are two big problems that keep scientists from clearly seeing the heavens. The lights from the cities are so bright that they wash out the lights from the stars. A bigger problem is the blanket of air that covers Earth. It blurs the view. The HST will overcome these problems. In space there are no clouds and no bright city lights.

The HST is a huge telescope. It is 43 feet long and 14 feet across. It weighs 24,250 pounds. It is very powerful, too. Scientists say that if you put a dime on the top of the Washington Monument in Washington, D.C., you would be able to clearly read the date on it from New York City using the HST. That is 175 miles away!

Directions: Answer these questions about a special telescope.

1. What is a telescope? ____________________

____

2. What is the name of the giant telescope that was launched into space in 1990?

____

3. What are two problems for scientists trying to look at the stars and planets from Earth?

____

4. How much does the HST weigh? ____________________

Name: ____________________

Space Pioneer

Neil Armstrong is one of the great pioneers of space. On July 20, 1969, Armstrong was commander of *Apollo 11*, the first manned American spacecraft to land on the Moon. He was the first person to walk on the Moon.

Armstrong was born in Ohio in 1930. He took his first airplane ride when he was 6 years old. As he grew older, he did jobs to earn money to learn to fly. On his 16th birthday, he received his student pilot's license.

Armstrong served as a Navy fighter pilot during the Korean War. He received three medals. Later, he was a test pilot. He was known as one of the best pilots in the world. He was also an engineer. He contributed much to the development of new methods of flying. In 1962, he was into an astronaut training program.

Armstrong had much experience when he was named to command the historic flight to the Moon. It took four days to fly to the Moon. As he climbed down the ladder to be the first person to step onto the Moon, he said these now famous words: "That's one small step for man, one giant leap for mankind."

Directions: Answer these questions about Neil Armstrong.

1. What did Neil Armstrong do before any other person in the world?

____

2. How old was Neil Armstrong when he got his student pilot's license?

____

3. What did Armstrong do during the Korean War?

____

4. On what date did a person first walk on the Moon?

____

Name: ____________________

Reading Comprehension: Amelia Earhart

More than 35 years before Neil Armstrong took that first step onto the surface of the Moon, another pioneer of the sky was becoming famous. Amelia Earhart was the first woman to fly around the world alone. She performed this amazing feat in 1932—2 years after Neil Armstrong was born.

Amelia saw an airplane for the first time at a fair when she was 8 years old. She was disappointed by the experience. She never would have dreamed that one day she would be a great pilot. Amelia didn't take her first plane ride for many years after that. But her first flight convinced her that she wanted to learn to fly. Her flying teacher, Neta Snook, was one of very few women at the time who knew how to fly. This inspired Amelia to learn to fly.

In 1927, she read about a man named Charles Lindbergh who became the first person to fly across the Atlantic Ocean alone. This was very dangerous at that time. In 1928, Amelia was a crew member of a plane that flew across the ocean. She was the first woman to do this. Four years later she made the trip on her own.

Amelia was very famous. The president called her an American heroine. Then, in 1937, Amelia decided to try to fly around the world at the equator. This had never been done before. Amelia never returned from the trip. To this day, no one knows for sure what happened to her. Many believe that she crashed into the ocean. But her failure was a challenge to others. She was indeed a great pioneer of the sky.

Directions: Answer these questions about Amelia Earhart.

1. What is the correct definition for **feat**?

   ☐ achievement ☐ trick ☐ flight

2. What is the correct definition for **inspired**?

   ☐ discouraged ☐ made to want to do ☐ frightened

3. How did Amelia Earhart feel the first time she saw an airplane? ____________________

4. Name the two things that Amelia Earhart was the first woman to achieve.

   a. ____________________

   b. ____________________

Name: ______________________

Reading Comprehension: Volcanoes

The volcano is one of the most amazing and frightening forces of nature. Maybe you have seen pictures of these "fireworks" of nature. Sometimes when a volcano erupts, a huge wall of melted rock creeps down its sides. It looks like a river of fire. Sometimes volcanoes explode, throwing the melted rock and ashes high into the air. But where does this melted rock come from?

The Earth is made up of many layers. The top layer is called the crust. Under the crust are many layers of hard rock. But far, far beneath the crust is rock so hot that it is soft. In some places it even melts. The melted rock is called magma. Sometimes the magma breaks out to the surface through cracks in the crust. These cracks are volcanoes.

Most people think of mountains when they think of volcanoes. But not every mountain is a volcano. A volcano is simply the opening in the earth from which the magma escapes. The hot magma, or lava cools and builds up on the surface of the Earth. Over thousands of years, this pile of cooled lava can grow to be very, very big. For example, the highest mountain in Africa, Kilimanjaro, is a volcano. It towers more than 16,000 feet above the ground around it.

Directions: Answer these questions about volcanoes.

1. What is the correct definition for **erupts**?

   ☐ drips out ☐ bursts out ☐ seeps out

2. What is the correct definition for **layer**?

   ☐ rocks ☐ a single thickness ☐ ground

3. What is the top layer of the earth called? ______________________

4. What is the word for hot magma that spills out of the Earth? ______________________

5. Where is the volcano called Kilimanjaro located? ______________________

Name: ____________________

Reading Comprehension: Oceans

If you looked at Earth from up in space, you would see a planet that is mostly blue. This is because more than two-thirds of Earth is covered with water. You already know that this is what makes our planet different from the others, and what makes life on Earth possible. Most of this water is in the four great oceans: Pacific, Atlantic, Indian and Arctic. The Pacific is by far the largest and the deepest. It is more than twice as big as the Atlantic, the second largest ocean.

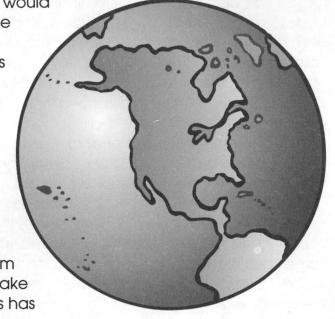

The water in the ocean is salty. This is because rivers are always pouring water into the oceans. Some of this water picks up salt from the rocks it flows over. It is not enough salt to make the rivers taste salty. But the salt in the oceans has been building up over millions of years. The oceans get more and more salty every century.

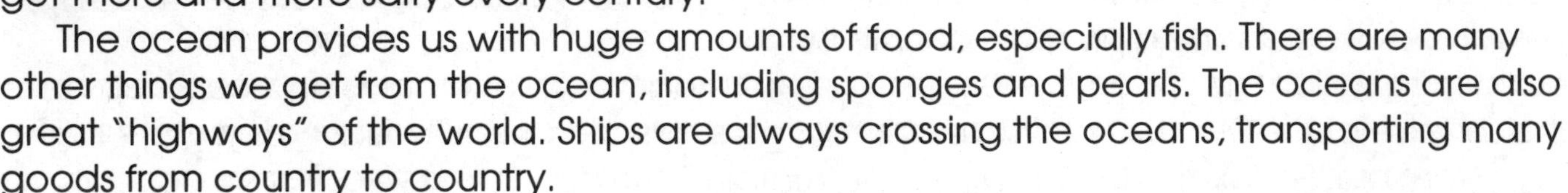
The ocean provides us with huge amounts of food, especially fish. There are many other things we get from the ocean, including sponges and pearls. The oceans are also great "highways" of the world. Ships are always crossing the oceans, transporting many goods from country to country.

The science of studying the ocean is called oceanography. Today, oceanographers have special equipment to help them learn about the oceans and seas. Electronic instruments can be sent deep below the surface to make measurements. The newest equipment uses sonar or echo-sounding systems that bounce sound waves off the sea bed and use the echoes to make pictures of the ocean floor.

Directions: Answer these questions about the oceans.

1. How much of the Earth is covered by water? ____________________
2. Which is the largest and deepest ocean? ____________________
3. What is the science of studying the ocean? ____________________
4. What new equipment do oceanographers use? ____________________

Name: ______________________

Reading Comprehension: Whales

The biggest animal in the world is the whale. The blue whale is the largest animal that ever lived. It is even bigger than the great dinosaurs of long ago. Whales are close cousins to dolphins and porpoises, but these animals are fewer than 13 feet in length.

Whales spend their entire lives in water, usually in the ocean. Because of this, many people think that whales are fish. They are not. They are mammals. There are four things that prove that whales are mammals instead of fish: 1) Whales breathe with lungs instead of gills. A whale must come to the surface to breathe. It blows the old air from its lungs out of a hole in the top of its head. 2) They are warm-blooded. 3) They have hair—though not very much! 4) Baby whales are born alive and get milk from their mothers.

Because whales often live in cold water, they have a thick layer of fat under their skin to protect them. This fat is called blubber. For many centuries, people have hunted the whale for its blubber.

Whales are very sociable animals and "talk" with each other by making different noises, including clicks, whistles, squeaks, thumps and low moans. Because sound waves travel well in water, the "song" of some whales can be heard more than 100 miles away.

Directions: Answer these questions about whales.

1. Which whale is the biggest animal that has ever lived? ______________________

2. List four things proving that whales are mammals and not fish.

   a. ______________________

   b. ______________________

   c. ______________________

   d. ______________________

3. What are two "cousins" to the whale? ______________________

4. What is the thick layer of fat under a whale's skin called? ______________________

Name: ____________________

Reading Comprehension: Dolphins and Porpoises

Dolphins and porpoises are members of the whale family. In fact, they are the most common whales. If they have pointed or "beaked" faces, they are dolphins. If they have short faces, they are porpoises. Sometimes large groups of more than 1,000 dolphins can be seen.

Dolphins and porpoises swim in a special way called "porpoising." They swim through the surface waters, diving down and then leaping up—sometimes into the air. As their heads come out of the water, they breathe in air. Dolphins are acrobatic swimmers, often spinning in the air as they leap.

Humans have always had a special relationship with dolphins. Stories dating back to the ancient Greeks talk about dolphins as friendly, helpful creatures. There have been reports over the years of people in trouble on the seas who have been rescued and helped by dolphins.

Directions: Answer these questions about dolphins and porpoises.

1. The small members of the whale family with the pointed faces are ____________.
2. Those members of the whale family with short faces are ____________.
3. What do you call the special way dolphins and porpoises swim? ____________.
4. Do dolphins breathe with lungs or gills? ____________
5. How did ancient Greeks describe dolphins? ____________
6. Where have dolphins been reported to help people? ____________

Name: ____________________

Reading Comprehension: Sharks

Sharks are known as the hunters of the sea. They are fish who eat other fish and even other sharks. Most people are frightened of sharks, but only a few of the more than 300 types of sharks are dangerous to people. Sharks vary in size and shape. The whale shark can be up to 60 feet long, but it is harmless. Some kinds of dogfish sharks are only a few inches long!

Sharks usually live in warm water, although they can be found anywhere in the ocean. Because of their shape, they are great swimmers.

Sharks are different from most other fish in a few ways. One important way is that they don't have any bones. Instead, their bodies have tough material called cartilage. Another way sharks are different is that their mouths are on the underside of the head. Most sharks have several rows of very sharp teeth. They never stop growing teeth. If a tooth wears out or is lost, a new one grows in its place.

Sharks spend most of their time eating and looking for food. They are excellent hunters. They can smell the smallest amount of blood from a long way off. Some kinds of sharks swim in packs, but the larger sharks hunt alone. Sharks usually approach their prey carefully, especially if it is big. Unless they are very hungry, they will swim around in a circle for some time before attacking. Experienced divers know how to swim with sharks and feed them. They can tell by the way a shark comes up to them if they should be afraid.

Directions: Answer these questions about sharks.

1.	Sharks are the hunters of the sea.	True	False
2.	There are thousands of kinds of sharks.	True	False
3.	All sharks are dangerous to humans.	True	False
4.	Sharks actually have very few teeth.	True	False
5.	Sharks spend most of their time eating and looking for food.	True	False

Name: ______________________

Reading Comprehension: Jacques Cousteau

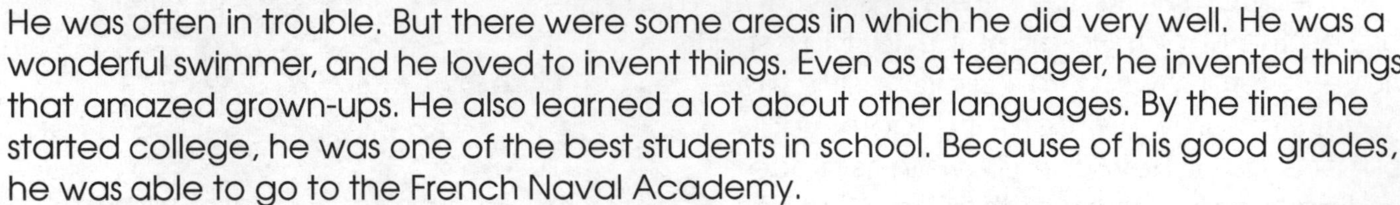

Jacques Cousteau was one of the most famous undersea explorers in history. He revolutionized this study with his inventions. His inventions include the aqua-lung and the diving saucer.

Jacques-Yves Cousteau was born in France in 1910. His family traveled a lot when he was a boy. They often visited the Atlantic Ocean. Even then, he was developing what would become a lifelong love for the sea.

Because of all the moving his family did, Cousteau was a poor student in school. He was often in trouble. But there were some areas in which he did very well. He was a wonderful swimmer, and he loved to invent things. Even as a teenager, he invented things that amazed grown-ups. He also learned a lot about other languages. By the time he started college, he was one of the best students in school. Because of his good grades, he was able to go to the French Naval Academy.

During World War II, Cousteau served as an officer in the French Navy. Most of his life became centered around the sea. He dreamed of owning his own ship. Finally, in 1950, he bought the *Calypso* (ca-LIP-so) and turned it into a research ship. Cousteau and his sailors explored the oceans. They searched shipwrecks and made underwater movies. He eventually won three Academy Awards for his undersea films. He also wrote many books about sea life. He worked very hard to teach people about the sea and how to take are of it.

Directions: Complete these statements about Jacques Cousteau.

1. Jacques Cousteau was born in ______________________.
2. As a boy, Cousteau liked to swim and to ______________________.
3. Cousteau's ship was called ______________________.
4. Cousteau's undersea films won him ______________________.

Name: ____________________

Reading Comprehension: Deep-Sea Diving

One part of the world is still largely unexplored. It is the deep sea. Over the years, many people have explored the sea. But the first deep-sea divers wanted to find sunken treasure. They weren't really interested in studying the creatures or life there. Only recently have they begun to learn some of the mysteries of the sea.

It's not easy to explore the deep sea. A diver must have a way of breathing under water. He must be able to protect himself from the terrific pressure. The pressure of air is about 15 pounds on every square inch. But the pressure of water is about 1,300 pounds on every square inch!

The first diving suits were made of rubber. They had a helmet of brass with windows in it. The shoes were made of lead and weighed 20 pounds each! These suits let divers go down a few hundred feet, but they were no good for exploring very deep waters. With a metal diving suit, a diver could go down 700 feet. Metal suits were first used in the 1930s.

In 1937, a diver named William Beebe wanted to explore deeper than anyone had ever gone before. He was not interested in finding treasure. He wanted to study deep-sea creatures and plants. He invented a hollow metal ball called the bathysphere. It weighed more than 5,000 pounds, but in it Beebe went down 3,028 feet. He saw many things that had never been seen by humans before.

Directions: Answer these questions about early deep-sea diving.

1. What were the first deep-sea divers interested in? ____________________

2. What are two problems that must be overcome in deep-sea diving?

   a. ____________________

   b. ____________________

3. How deep could a diver go wearing a metal suit? ____________________

4. Who was the deep-sea explorer who invented the bathysphere?

   ____

Name: ____________________

Reading Comprehension: Occupations

Directions: Read this article about coaching. Then answer the questions below.

When you see your coach at the practice field or in a game, you are seeing only a small part of your coach's life. Your coach has to spend a great deal of time even before your season begins. He/she needs to attend meetings so that the teams can be divided into groups. Each coach in the conference (a group of teams that are scheduled to play each other) has to attend more meetings—this time to set up the dates they will have games.

Your coach, whether it is a man or a woman, usually has a job to go to every day. The time he/she spends with you and your team mates means that he/she has even less time to spend with friends and family. Your coach feels it is important to help you learn how to play and to learn good sportsmanship.

The next time you sign up for a sport, look at your coach with a "different set of eyes." Always do your best, be a good team player and remember to thank your coach for all that he/she does!

1. What is a conference? ____________________

____

2. What does it mean to look at your coach with a "different set of eyes"?

____

____

3. Name one way you can show your coach you appreciate him/her.

____

Name: ______________________

Reading Comprehension: Occupations

Directions: Read this story about artistic people. Then answer the questions below.

Are you a good artist? Do you like to draw? Some people like to sit and "doodle" when they are listening to the radio, watching television or talking on the telephone. You might have noticed these little cartoons or designs written on the message pad by your phone. (The "doodler" has been here!)

It is true that people like their occupations better if they are doing something they enjoy. It would not be much fun to be a great artist and have to work as a bus driver or a store clerk. These are some of the jobs you could have if you were a good artist: book illustrator, greeting card artist, art teacher, movie animator, cartoonist for magazines or newspapers.

1. What is a "doodler"? ______________________

2. Read the list of five possible occupations for an artist. Pretend you are an artist. Which job would you choose? Why? ______________________

____

____

____

MASTER SKILLS
READING 4

Name: ____________________

Reading Skills: Advertisements

Stores pay for advertisements, or ads, to let people know what is being sold. You see ads in newspapers and magazines, and on television and radio.

Directions: Use the following newspaper ad to answer the questions.

Home Cooking Restaurant
Open Easter Sunday 10:30 a.m. to 8:00 p.m.
Special Easter Menu
• Roast Turkey $10.50
• Baked Ham $12.00
• Roast Leg of Lamb $15.50
Many other dishes available, including veal, chicken, seafood and pasta.
Call for reservations 555–6241
Home Cooking Restaurant
1485 City Street

1. The restaurant is advertising special holiday meals. What holiday are they for?

   ____

2. What is the most expensive meal listed on the menu? ____________________

3. What hours will the restaurant be open on Easter? ____________________

Name: ______________________

Reading Skills: Advertisements

Directions: Use the following newspaper ad to answer the questions.

New-Look Fashions

Final Week!
Spring Suit Sale

Buy one suit at the regular price and get a second one for only $50!

Suits: From $75 to $150

New-Look Fashions
5290 Main Street

Hours: Monday–Friday 10–7; Saturday 10–6; Closed Sunday

1. What is the regular price for a suit? ______________________
2. If you buy one suit at the regular price, what is the price for a second one?

   ____
3. What day is the store closed? ______________________
4. What hours is the store open on Wednesday? ______________________
5. When is the sale? ______________________

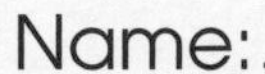

Reading Skills: Advertisements

Directions: Use the following newspaper ad to answer the questions.

House of Plants

Colorful Flowering Trees

Flowering Crab Apple Trees
Sizes up to 10 ft.
Beautiful Colored Spring Flowers
Dark Green Foliage
Red, Pink, White Blossoms

25% OFF

Reg. $29.99 to $149.99
NOW $22.49 to $112.50

House of Plants
6280 River Road

1. How big are the biggest flowering crab apple trees for sale?

____

2. What are the regular prices?

____

3. What are the sale prices?

____

Name: 

Reading Skills: Bus Schedules

Schedules are important to our daily lives. Your parents' jobs, school, even watching television—all are based on schedules. When you travel, you probably follow a schedule, too. Most forms of public transportation, such as subways, buses and trains, run on schedules. These "timetables" tell passengers when they will leave each stop or station.

Directions: Use the following city bus schedule to answer the questions.

No. 2 Cross-Town Bus Schedule

State St. at Park Way	Oak St. at Green Ave.	Fourth St. at Ninth Ave.	Buyall Shopping Center
5:00 a.m.	5:14 a.m.	5:23 a.m.	5:30 a.m.
6:38	6:52	7:01	7:08
7:50	8:05	8:14	8:21
9:04	9:18	9:27	9:34
10:15	10:29	10:38	10:47
12:20 p.m.	12:34 p.m.	12:43 p.m.	12:50 p.m.
1:46	2:00	2:09	2:16
3:30	3:44	3:53	4:00
5:20	5:34	5:43	5:50
6:02	6:16	6:25	6:32

1. The first bus of the day leaves the State St./Park Way stop at 5 a.m. What time does the last bus of the day leave this stop? ____________

2. The bus that leaves the Oak St./Green Ave. stop at 8:05 a.m. leaves the Buyall Shopping Center at what time? ____________

3. What time does the first afternoon bus leave the Fourth St./Ninth Ave. stop? ____________

4. How many buses each day run between the State St./Park Way stop and the Buyall Shopping Center? ____________

Name: 

Reading Skills: Train Schedules

Directions: Below is part of a schedule for trains leaving New York City for cities all around the country. Use the schedule to answer the questions.

Destination	Train Number	Departure Time	Arrival Time
Birmingham	958	9:00 a.m.	12:31 a.m.
Boston	611	7:15 a.m.	4:30 p.m.
Cambridge	398	8:15 a.m.	1:14 p.m.
Cincinnati	242	5:00 a.m.	7:25 p.m.
Detroit	415	1:45 p.m.	4:40 a.m.
Evansville	623	3:00 p.m.	8:28 a.m.

1. What is the number of the train that leaves latest in the day? ____________
2. What city is the destination for train number 623? ____________
3. What time does the train for Boston leave New York? ____________
4. What time does train number 415 arrive in Detroit? ____________
5. What is the destination of the train that leaves earliest in the day? ____________

Name: ______________________

Reading Skills: Labels

Directions: You should never take any medicine without your parents' permission, but it is good to know how to read the label of a medicine bottle. Read the label to answer the questions.

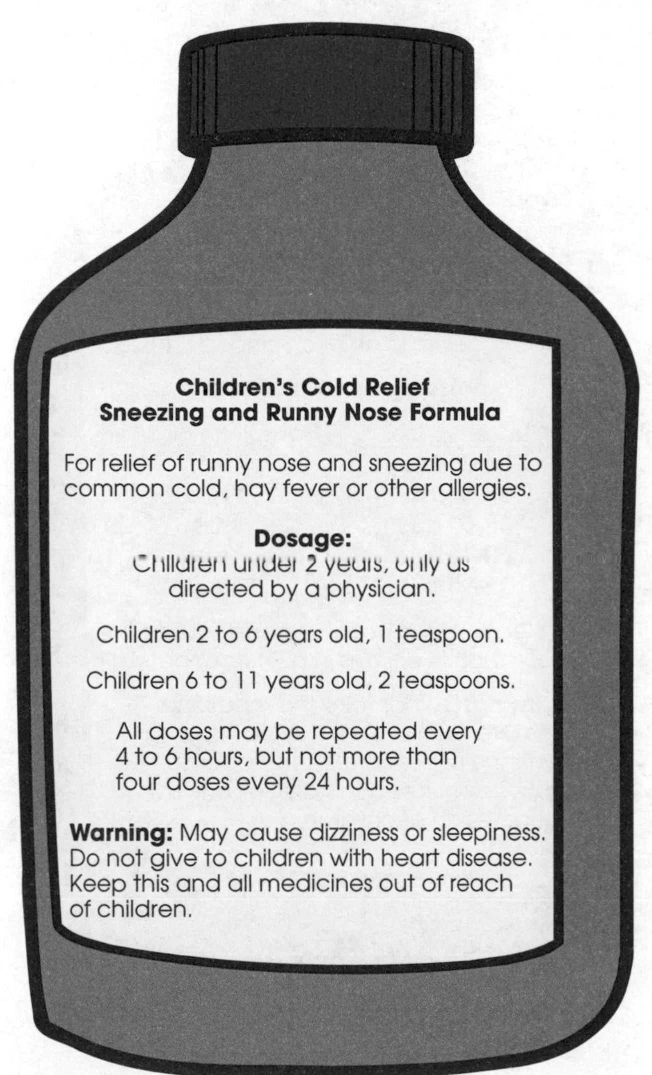

Children's Cold Relief
Sneezing and Runny Nose Formula
For relief of runny nose and sneezing due to common cold, hay fever or other allergies.
Dosage:
Children under 2 years, only as directed by a physician.
Children 2 to 6 years old, 1 teaspoon.
Children 6 to 11 years old, 2 teaspoons.
All doses may be repeated every 4 to 6 hours, but not more than four doses every 24 hours.
Warning: May cause dizziness or sleepiness. Do not give to children with heart disease. Keep this and all medicines out of reach of children.

1. How much medicine should a 5 year old take? ______________________
2. How often can this medicine be taken? ______________________
3. How do you know how much medicine to give a 1 year old? ______________________
4. Who should not take this medicine? ______________________

MASTER SKILLS
READING 4

Name: ____________________

Reading Skills: Labels

Directions: Use the following medicine bottle label to answer the questions.

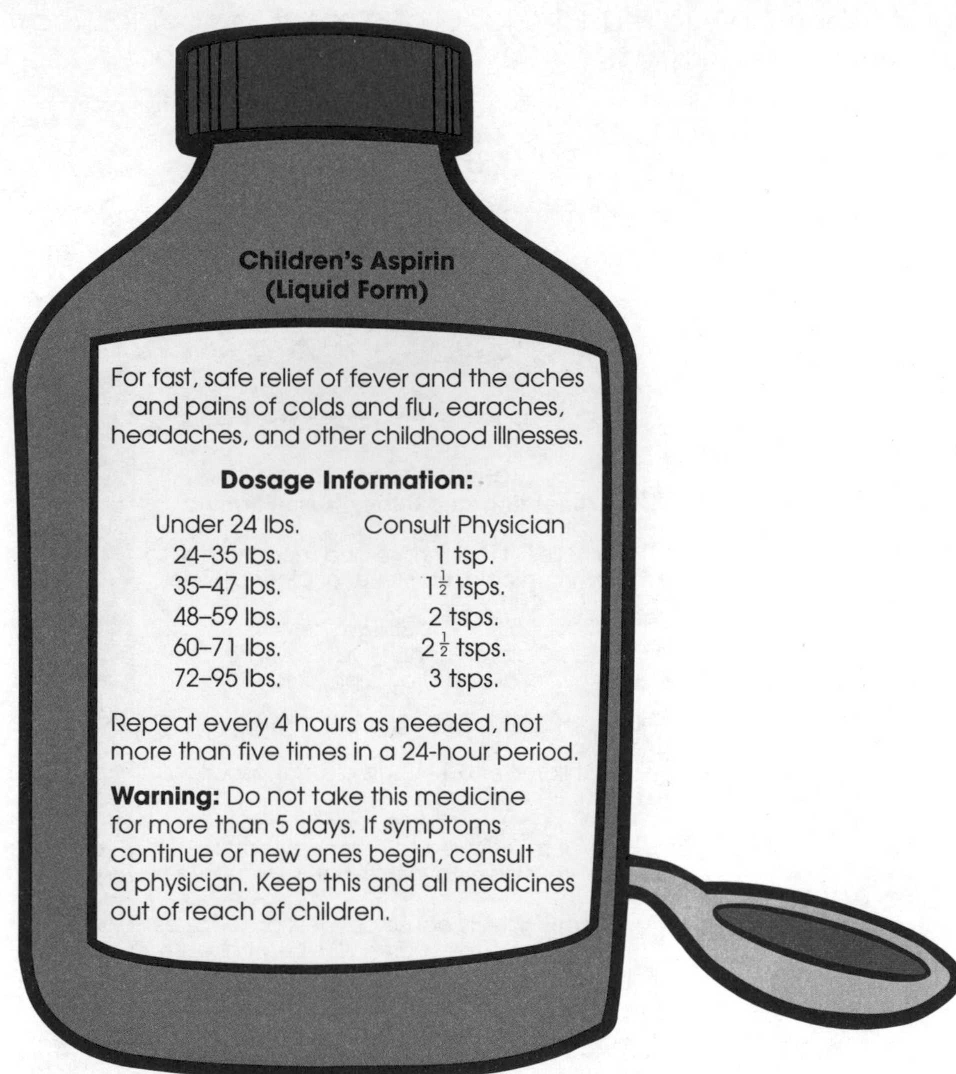
Children's Aspirin
(Liquid Form)
For fast, safe relief of fever and the aches and pains of colds and flu, earaches, headaches, and other childhood illnesses.
Dosage Information:
Under 24 lbs. Consult Physician
24–35 lbs. 1 tsp.
35–47 lbs. $1\frac{1}{2}$ tsps.
48–59 lbs. 2 tsps.
60–71 lbs. $2\frac{1}{2}$ tsps.
72–95 lbs. 3 tsps.
Repeat every 4 hours as needed, not more than five times in a 24-hour period.
Warning: Do not take this medicine for more than 5 days. If symptoms continue or new ones begin, consult a physician. Keep this and all medicines out of reach of children.

1. Circle the correct meaning of **dosage**.
   the kind of medicine
   the amount of medicine to give at one time
   the person who takes the medicine

2. What is the correct dosage for a child weighing 51 pounds? ____________________

3. Underline the correct meaning of **warning**.
   something that tells you of danger
   the instructions for how much medicine to give
   the person who takes the medicine

Name: ______________________

Review

Directions: Use the following "Help Wanted" ads to answer the questions.

Baby-sitter. Caring, responsible person needed to take care of 2 and 4 year old in our home. 25–30 hours per week. Must have own transportation. References required. Call 725-1342 after 7 p.m.

Clerk/Typist. Law firm seeks part-time help. Duties include typing, filing and answering telephone. Monday–Friday, 1–6 p.m. Previous experience preferred. Apply in person. 1392 E. Long St.

Driver for Disabled. Van provided. Includes some evenings and Saturdays. No experience necessary. Call Mike at 769-1533.

Head Nurse. Join in the bloodmobile team at the American Red Cross. Full- and part-time positions available. Great benefits. Apply Monday thru Friday 9–4. 1495 N. State St.

Teachers. For new child-care program. Prefer degree in Early Childhood Development and previous experience. Must be non-smoker. Call 291-5555.

1. For which job would you have to work some evenings and Saturdays?

____

2. Which job calls for a person who does not smoke?

____

3. For which job would you have to have your own transportation?

____

4. For which job must you apply in person?

____

5. Which ad offers both part-time and full-time positions?

____

Glossary

Analogy: A way of comparing things to show how they are similar. Example: Nose is to smell as tongue is to taste.

Antonym: A word that means the opposite of another word. Example: **in** and **out**.

Classifying: Placing similar things into categories.

Context: The other words in the sentence or the sentences before or after a word.

Context Clues: A way to figure out the meaning of a word by relating it to other words in the sentence.

Fact: A statement that can be proven true.

Homophones: Two words that sound the same, but have different meanings and are usually spelled differently. Example: **write** and **right**.

Main Idea: The most important idea, or main points, in a sentence, paragraph or story.

Opinion: A statement that tells how someone feels or what he/she thinks about something or someone.

Prefix: A syllable at the beginning of a word that changes its meaning.

Sequencing: Putting items or events in logical order.

Suffix: A syllable at the end of a word that changes its meaning.

Syllable: Part of a word. Each syllable has one vowel sound.

Synonym: A word that means the same, or nearly the same, as another word. Example: **brave** and **courageous**.

Venn Diagram: A diagram used to chart information that shows similarities and differences between two things.

Answer Keys

Vocabulary: Synonyms

A **synonym** is a word that means the same, or nearly the same, as another word.
Example: quick and **fast**

Directions: Draw lines to match the words in Column A with their synonyms in Column B.

Column A	Column B
plain	unusual
career	vocation
rare	disappear
vanish	greedy
beautiful	finish
selfish	simple
complete	lovely

Directions: Choose a word from Column A or Column B to complete each sentence below.

Sample answers:

1. Dad was very excited when he discovered the rare/unusual coin for sale on the display counter.
2. My dog is a real magician; he can vanish/disappear into thin air when he sees me getting his bath ready!
3. Many of my classmates joined the discussion about career/vocation choices we had considered.
4. "You will need to finish/complete your report on ancient Greece before you sign up for computer time," said Mr. Rastetter.
5. Your beautiful/lovely painting will be on display in the art show.

3

Vocabulary: Synonyms

tired greedy easy rough minute melted friend smart

Directions: For each sentence, choose a word from the box that is a synonym for the bold word. Write the synonym above the word.

1. Boy, this road is really **bumpy**! (rough)
2. The operator said politely, "One **moment**, please." (minute)
3. My parents are usually **exhausted** when they get home from work. (tired)
4. "Don't be so **selfish**! Can't you share with us?" asked Rob. (greedy)
5. That puzzle was actually quite **simple**. (easy)
6. "Who's your **buddy**?" Dad asked as we walked onto the porch. (friend)
7. When it comes to animals, my Uncle Steve is quite **intelligent**. (smart)
8. The frozen treat **thawed** while I stood in line for the bus. (melted)

4

Vocabulary: Synonyms

Directions: For each paragraph, choose a word from the box that is a synonym for each bold word. Write the synonym above the word.

manual beautiful simple wonderful greatest finished

Danielle and Mackenzie worked hard to earn the **best** (greatest) badge for Girl Scouts. Each knew that her **workbook** (manual) had to be **completed** (finished) by the meeting on Saturday. Danielle's mother suggested that they work at the park and change it from a **plain** (simple) setting to something more **lovely** (beautiful). The girls agreed that Danielle's mother had a **great** (wonderful) idea to help them earn the environmental badge.

beside tired evening important competition hopped

The two boys **jumped** (hopped) on their bikes and headed down the hill toward the park. Corey and Justin knew that they needed to be at ball practice today or they would be unable to play in the **game** (competition) Friday **night** (evening). They had worked all day in the fields **alongside** (beside) their father. They were **exhausted** (tired), but knew that it was **crucial** (important) that they not be late.

5

Vocabulary: Antonyms

An **antonym** is a word that means the opposite of another word.
Example: difficult and **easy**

Directions: Choose words from the box to complete the crossword puzzle.

friend vanish quit safety liquids scatter help noisy

ACROSS:
2. Opposite of **gather** — SCATTER
3. Opposite of **enemy** — FRIEND
4. Opposite of **prevent** — HELP
6. Opposite of **begin** — QUIT
7. Opposite of **silent** — NOISY

DOWN:
1. Opposite of **appear** — VANISH
2. Opposite of **danger** — SAFETY
5. Opposite of **solids** — LIQUIDS

6

Vocabulary: Antonyms

Directions: Each bold word below has an antonym in the box. Use these words to write new sentences. The first one is done for you.

friend vanish quit safety liquids help scatter worse

1. I'll help you **gather** all the papers on the lawn.
   The strong winds will scatter the leaves.
2. The fourth graders were learning about the many **solids** in their classroom.
   Answer should include "liquids."
3. "It's time to **begin** our lesson on the continents," said Ms. Haynes.
   Answer should include "quit."
4. "That's strange. The stapler decided to **appear** all of a sudden," said Mr. Jonson.
   Answer should include "vanish."
5. The doctor said this new medicine should **prevent** colds.
   Answer should include "help."
6. "She is our **enemy**, boys, we can't let her in our clubhouse!" cried Paul.
   Answer should include "friend."
7. I'm certain that dark cave is full of **danger**!
   Answer should include "safety."
8. Give me a chance to make the situation **better**.
   Answer should include "worse."

7

Vocabulary: Synonyms and Antonyms

Directions: Use the words in the box to write a synonym for each word below. Write it next to the S. Next to the A, write an antonym. The first one is done for you.

appear, under, embarrassed, icy, proud, melted, gloomy, valuable, merry, unnecessary, bent, immediate, straight, late, break, old, repair, new, fancy, bumpy, plain, smooth, above, vanish

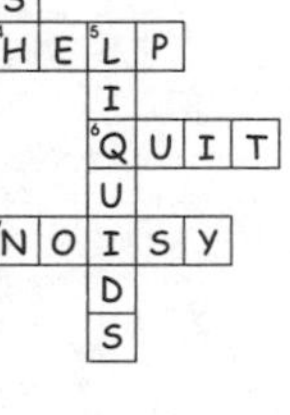

1. crooked — S: bent; A: straight
2. frozen — S: icy; A: melted
3. instant — S: immediate; A: late
4. damage — S: break; A: repair
5. important — S: valuable; A: unnecessary
6. ashamed — S: embarrassed; A: proud
7. cheerful — S: merry; A: gloomy
8. elegant — S: fancy; A: plain
9. rough — S: bumpy; A: smooth
10. beneath — S: under; A: above
11. disappear — S: vanish; A: appear
12. ancient — S: old; A: new

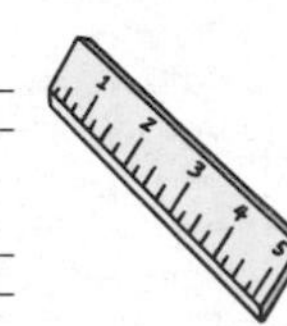

8

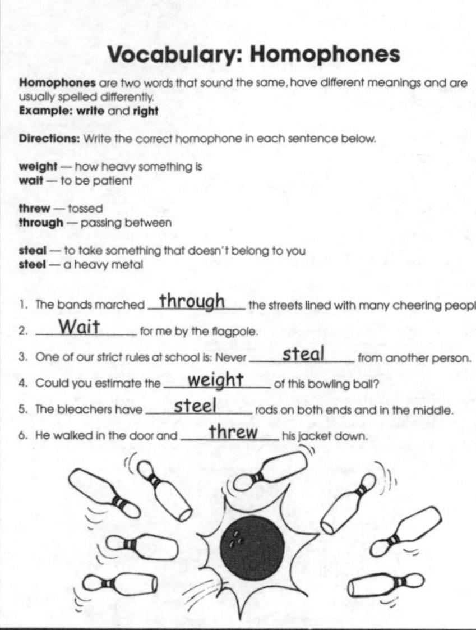

Vocabulary: Homophones

Homophones are two words that sound the same, have different meanings and are usually spelled differently.
Example: write and **right**

Directions: Write the correct homophone in each sentence below.

weight — how heavy something is
wait — to be patient

threw — tossed
through — passing between

steal — to take something that doesn't belong to you
steel — a heavy metal

1. The bands marched through the streets lined with many cheering people.
2. Wait for me by the flagpole.
3. One of our strict rules at school is: Never steal from another person.
4. Could you estimate the weight of this bowling ball?
5. The bleachers have steel rods on both ends and in the middle.
6. He walked in the door and threw his jacket down.

9

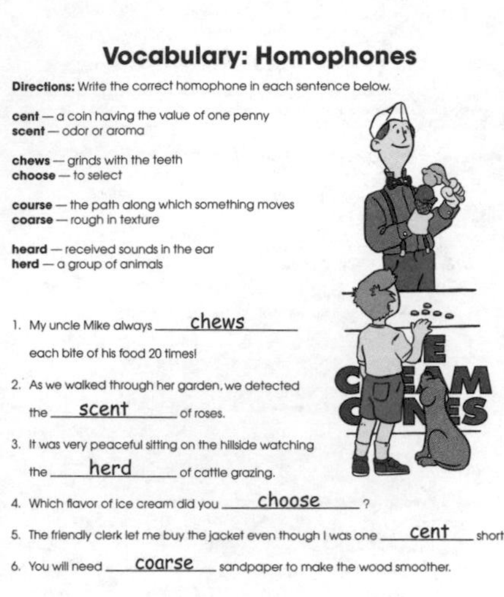

Vocabulary: Homophones

Directions: Write the correct homophone in each sentence below.

cent — a coin having the value of one penny
scent — odor or aroma

chews — grinds with the teeth
choose — to select

course — the path along which something moves
coarse — rough in texture

heard — received sounds in the ear
herd — a group of animals

1. My uncle Mike always chews each bite of his food 20 times!
2. As we walked through her garden, we detected the scent of roses.
3. It was very peaceful sitting on the hillside watching the herd of cattle grazing.
4. Which flavor of ice cream did you choose?
5. The friendly clerk let me buy the jacket even though I was one cent short.
6. You will need coarse sandpaper to make the wood smoother.

10

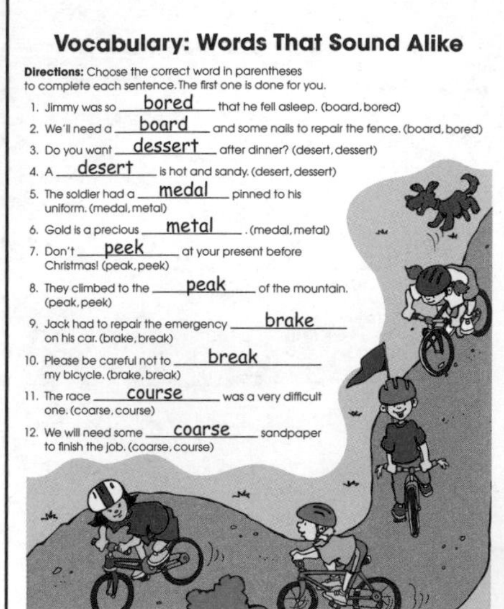

Vocabulary: Words That Sound Alike

Directions: Choose the correct word in parentheses to complete each sentence. The first one is done for you.

1. Jimmy was so bored that he fell asleep. (board, bored)
2. We'll need a board and some nails to repair the fence. (board, bored)
3. Do you want dessert after dinner? (desert, dessert)
4. A desert is hot and sandy. (desert, dessert)
5. The soldier had a medal pinned to his uniform. (medal, metal)
6. Gold is a precious metal. (medal, metal)
7. Don't peek at your present before Christmas! (peak, peek)
8. They climbed to the peak of the mountain. (peak, peek)
9. Jack had to repair the emergency brake on his car. (brake, break)
10. Please be careful not to break my bicycle. (brake, break)
11. The race course was a very difficult one. (coarse, course)
12. We will need some coarse sandpaper to finish the job. (coarse, course)

11

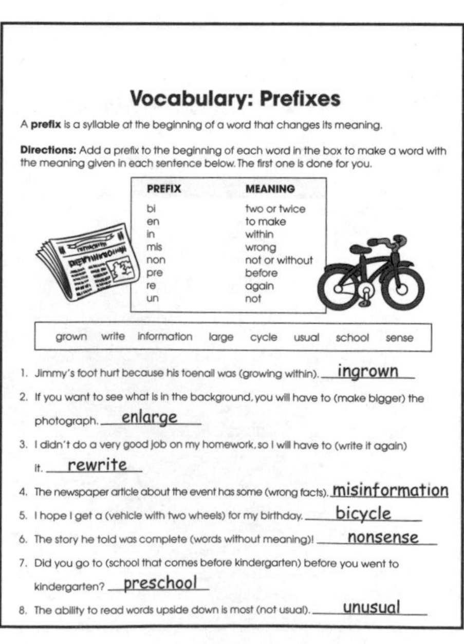

Vocabulary: Prefixes

A **prefix** is a syllable at the beginning of a word that changes its meaning.

Directions: Add a prefix to the beginning of each word in the box to make a word with the meaning given in each sentence below. The first one is done for you.

PREFIX	MEANING
bi	two or twice
en	to make
in	within
mis	wrong
non	not or without
pre	before
re	again
un	not

grown write information large cycle usual school sense

1. Jimmy's foot hurt because his toenail was (growing within). ingrown
2. If you want to see what is in the background, you will have to (make bigger) the photograph. enlarge
3. I didn't do a very good job on my homework, so I will have to (write it again) it. rewrite
4. The newspaper article about the event has some (wrong facts). misinformation
5. I hope I get a (vehicle with two wheels) for my birthday. bicycle
6. The story he told was complete (words without meaning)! nonsense
7. Did you go to (school that comes before kindergarten) before you went to kindergarten? preschool
8. The ability to read words upside down is most (not usual). unusual

12

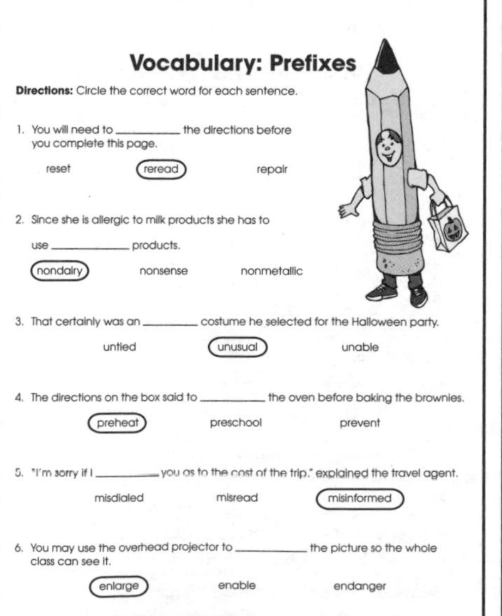

Vocabulary: Prefixes

Directions: Circle the correct word for each sentence.

1. You will need to ______ the directions before you complete this page.
   reset (reread) repair
2. Since she is allergic to milk products she has to use ______ products.
   (nondairy) nonsense nonmetallic
3. That certainly was an ______ costume he selected for the Halloween party.
   untied (unusual) unable
4. The directions on the box said to ______ the oven before baking the brownies.
   (preheat) preschool prevent
5. "I'm sorry if I ______ you as to the cost of the trip," explained the travel agent.
   misdialed misread (misinformed)
6. You may use the overhead projector to ______ the picture so the whole class can see it.
   (enlarge) enable endanger

13

Vocabulary: Suffixes

A **suffix** is a syllable at the end of a word that changes its meaning. In most cases, when adding a suffix that begins with a vowel, drop the final **e** of the root word. For example, **fame** becomes **famous**. Also, change a final **y** in the root word to **i** before adding any suffix except **ing**. For example, **silly** becomes **silliness**.

Directions: Add a suffix to the end of each word in the box to make a word with the meaning given (in parentheses) in each sentence below. The first one is done for you.

SUFFIX	MEANING
ful	full of
ity	quality or degree
ive	have or tend to be
less	without or lacking
able	able to be
ness	state of
ment	act of
or	person that does something
ward	in the direction of

effect like thought pay beauty thank back act happy

1. Mike was (full of thanks) for a hot meal. thankful
2. I was (without thinking) for forgetting your birthday. thoughtless
3. The mouse trap we put out doesn't seem to be (have an effect). effective
4. In spring, the flower garden is (full of beauty). beautiful
5. Sally is such a (able to be liked) girl! likable
6. Tim fell over (in the direction of the back) because he wasn't watching where he was going. backward
7. Jill's wedding day was one of great (the state of being happy). happiness
8. The (person who performs) was very good in the play. actor
9. I have to make a (act of paying) for the stereo I bought. payment

14

Vocabulary: Suffixes

Directions: Read the story. Choose the correct word from the box to complete the sentences.

beautiful	colorful	payment
breakable	careful	backward
careless	director	agreement
basement	forward	firmness

Colleen and Marj carried the boxes down to the basement apartment. "Be careful with those," cautioned Colleen's mother. "All the things in that box are breakable." As soon as the two girls helped carry all the boxes from the moving van down the stairs, they would be able to go to school for the play tryouts. That was the agreement made with Colleen's mother earlier that day.

"It won't do any good to get careless with your work. Just keep at it and the job will be done quickly," she spoke with a firmness in her voice.

"It's hard to see where I'm going when I have to walk backward," groaned Marj. "Can we switch places with the next box?"

Colleen agreed to switch places, but they soon discovered that the last two boxes were lightweight. Each girl had her own box to carry, so each of them got to walk looking forward. "These are so light," remarked Marj. "What's in them?"

"These have the beautiful, colorful hats I was telling you about. We can take them to the play tryouts with us," answered Colleen. "I bet we'll impress the director. Even if we don't get parts in the play, I bet our hats will!"

Colleen's mother handed each of the girls a 5-dollar bill. "I really appreciate your help. Will this be enough?"

"Thanks, Mom. You bet!" Colleen shouted as the girls ran down the sidewalk.

15

Vocabulary: Parts of the Body

Directions: Unscramble the remaining letters of each word that names a part of the body. Then write each word in the sentence that describes it. The first one is done for you.

anirb brain
noteug tongue
rilev liver
skidyen kidneys
gluns lungs
erath heart
shoctam stomach

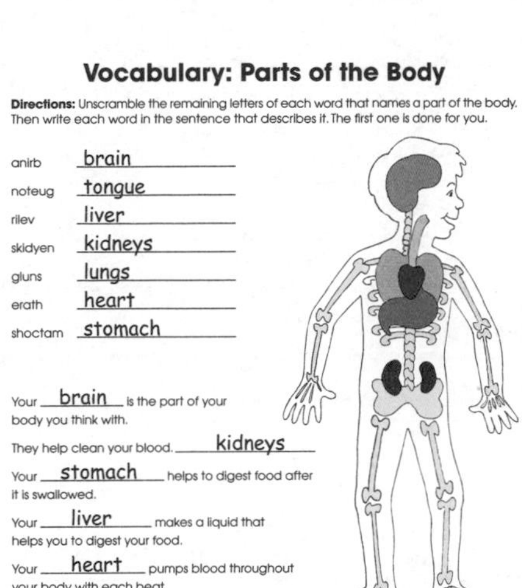

Your brain is the part of your body you think with.

They help clean your blood. kidneys

Your stomach helps to digest food after it is swallowed.

Your liver makes a liquid that helps you to digest your food.

Your heart pumps blood throughout your body with each beat.

Your lungs are filled with air when you breathe.

Your tongue is the muscle in your mouth that helps you talk and taste.

16

Vocabulary: Occupations

Directions: Unscramble the bold words to write the title of the person who does the described job. The first one is done for you.

1. A **inacimus** writes, sings or plays music. musician
2. An **trasotanu** is trained to fly a spaceship. astronaut
3. An **itrode** prepares other people's writing to be printed in a book, newspaper or magazine. editor
4. An **rigeenen** operates an engine, such as on a train. engineer
5. An **brocata** performs gymnastic or tumbling exercises that use control of the body. acrobat
6. A **ilaort** makes clothing for people. tailor
7. A **veecitted** works to get information, especially about crimes or suspicious people. detective
8. A **tissicent** works and performs experiments in one of the sciences, such as chemistry. scientist
9. An **sattir** makes beautiful things, such as paintings and statues. artist
10. A **hocca** teaches and trains students, especially in sports. coach
11. An **rotac** performs in plays or movies. actor
12. A **suner** is trained to care for sick people and to assist doctors. nurse
13. A **naicigam** is a performer skilled in magic tricks. magician

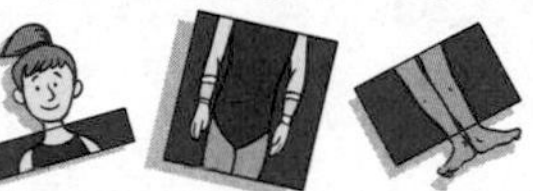

17

Vocabulary: Occupations

Directions: Find each word from the box in the word search and circle it. Words may go across, down, diagonal or backward.

magician scientist coach astronaut musician acrobat tailor
engineer nurse detective actor artist editor

m	a	g	i	c	i	a	n	d	o	a	s
u	a	r	m	p	v	c	u	e	j	a	c
s	p	y	g	t	o	t	r	t	n	p	i
i	l	s	t	b	k	o	s	e	r	a	e
c	o	a	c	h	e	r	e	c	e	s	n
i	u	l	t	m	d	t	n	t	d	t	t
a	c	r	o	b	a	t	g	i	i	r	i
n	k	t	y	i	o	j	i	v	t	o	s
o	p	n	l	f	t	r	n	e	o	n	t
a	b	o	l	l	c	i	e	d	r	a	n
c	r	d	d	m	p	e	e	f	f	u	a
p	e	e	t	s	i	t	r	a	r	t	j

Directions: Draw a line between each job and the word that best goes with it.

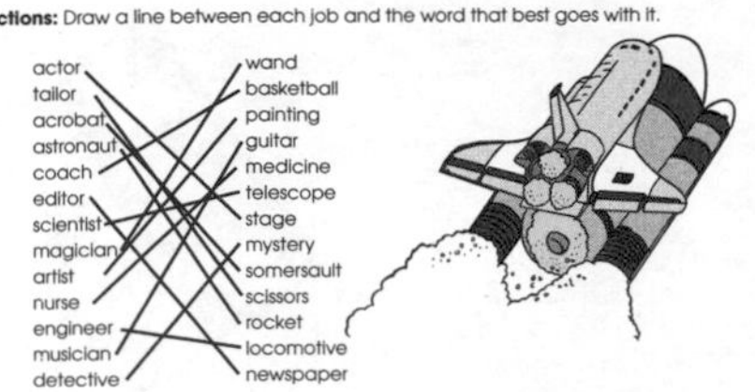

18

Vocabulary: Sports

Directions: Find each word in the word search. Then unscramble the bold words in the sentences below.

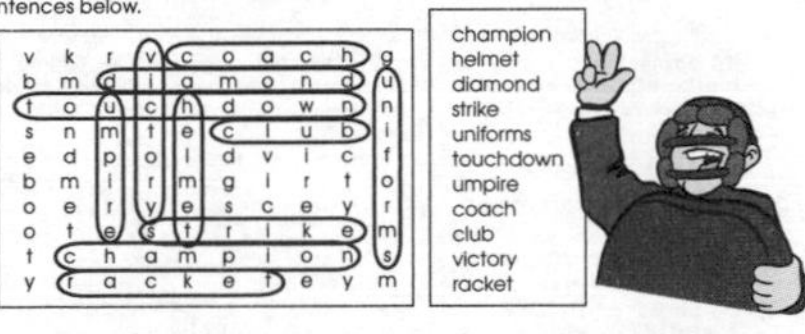

1. A football player wears a **melteh** to protect his head. helmet
2. If our team wins tonight, it will be our tenth **rticoyv** this year. victory
3. When it rained, they put a cover over the baseball **middona**. diamond
4. Our **hacco** asked us to stay after school to practice. coach
5. With only a minute left in the football game, Jimmy scored the winning **wontcudoh**. touchdown
6. In golf, you hit the ball with a **bluc**. club
7. Do all boxing fans know the name of the heavy-weight **miocpahn**? champion
8. I thought I tagged the base, but the **mipure** said I was out. umpire
9. In tennis, you hit the ball with a **rcatek**. racket
10. If we earn enough money selling candy, our team will get new **nifmorus**. uniforms
11. I bet our best pitcher can **trekis** out your best hitter. strike

19

Reading Skills: Context Clues

When you read, you may confuse words that look alike. You can tell when you read a word incorrectly because it doesn't make sense. You can tell from the **context** (the other words in the sentence or the sentences before or after) what the word should be. These **context clues** can help you figure out the meaning of a word by relating it to other words in the sentence.

Directions: Circle the correct word for each sentence below. Use the context to help you.

1. We knew we were in trouble as soon as we heard the crash. The baseball had gone (through, thought) the picture window!
2. She was not able to answer my question because her (month, mouth) was full of pizza.
3. Asia is the largest continent in the (world, word).
4. I'm not sure I heard the teacher correctly. Did he say what I (through, thought) he said?
5. I was not with them on vacation so I don't know a (think, thing) about what happened.
6. My favorite (month, mouth) of the year is July because I love fireworks and parades!
7. You will do better on your book report if you (think, thing) about what you are going to say.

20

Reading Skills: Context Clues

Directions: Read each sentence carefully and circle the word that makes sense.

1. We didn't (except, expect) you to arrive so early.
2. "I can't hear a (word, world) you are saying. Wait until I turn down the stereo," said Val.
3. I couldn't sleep last night because of the (noise, nose) from the apartment below us.
4. Did Peggy say (weather, whether) or not we needed our binoculars for the game?
5. He broke his (noise, nose) when he fell off the bicycle.
6. All the students (except, expect) the four in the front row are excused to leave.
7. The teacher said we should have good (whether, weather) for our field trip.

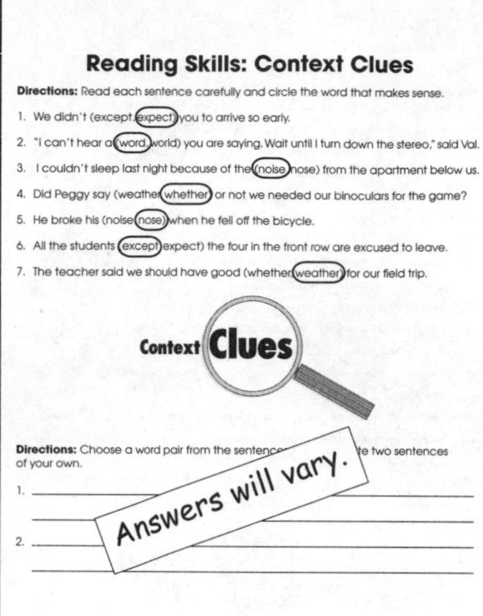

Directions: Choose a word pair from the sentences ... te two sentences of your own.

1. ______
2. ______

21

Reading Skills: Context Clues

Directions: Use context clues to figure out the bold word in each sentence below.

1. The teacher wanted all of us to put the names of the students in our class in two **columns**. It was a big help when I saw how she started each list on the board.
2. "I'm glad to see such a **variety** of art projects at the display," said the principal. "I was afraid that many of the projects would be the same."
3. My father used to work for a huge **corporation** in Florida. Since we moved to Virginia, his job is with a smaller company.
4. It would be hard to come up with a **singular** reason for the football team's success. There are so many good things happening that could explain it.

Directions: Draw a line to match the word on the left with its definition on the right.

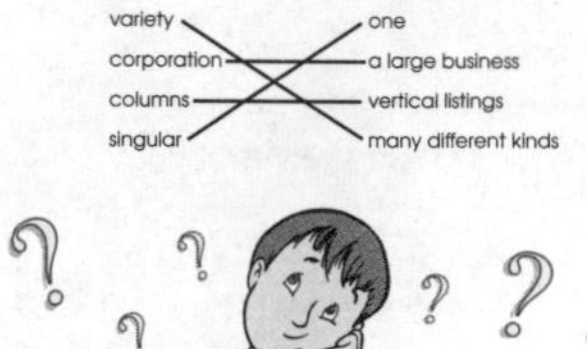

22

Reading Skills: Context Clues

Directions: Use context clues to help you choose the correct word for each sentence below.

selected match scarecrow

Diane and Donna are twin sisters. The clothes they wear nearly always match. At school one day, Donna's teacher selected one of the students to dress up as a scarecrow for the fall harvest play. She chose Donna. Everyone was quite surprised the night of the play. Donna was not the only scarecrow. Diane looked the part, too!

problem driver intersection

Dad sometimes works very late. This caused a problems on his way home last night. As he was approaching the intersection near our home, he started to fall asleep! The whole family was very glad that the driver in the car behind Dad honked his car horn to wake him up.

cancel decision storm

"It looks very much like it could storm tonight," said Brent. Rob replied, "Are you saying we should cancel our game?" "Let's not make a decision just yet," answered Brent.

23

Reading Skills: Context Clues

Directions: Use context clues to help you choose the correct word for each sentence below.

designs studying collection

Our fourth-grade class will be studying castles for the next four weeks. Mrs. Oswalt will be helping with our study. She plans to share her collection of castle models with the class. We are all looking forward to our morning in the sand at the school's volleyball court. We all get to try our own designs to see how they work.

breath excited quietly

Michelle was very excited the other day when she came into the classroom. We all noticed that she had trouble sitting quietly in her seat until it was her turn to share with us. When her turn finally came, she took a deep breath and told us that her mom was going to have a baby!

responsibility chooses messages

Each week, our teacher chooses classroom helpers. They get to be part of the Job Squad. Some helpers have the responsibility of watering the plants. Everyone's favorite job is when they get to take messages to the office or to another teacher's room.

24

Reading Skills: Context Clues

Directions: Read the story. Match each bold word with its definition below.

Where the northern shores of North America meet the Arctic Ocean, the winters are very long and cold. No plants or crops will grow there. This is the land of the **Eskimo**.

Eskimos have figured out ways to live in the snow and ice. They sometimes live in **igloos**, which are made of snow. It is really very comfortable inside! An oil lamp provides light and warmth.

Often, you will find a big, furry **husky** sleeping in the long tunnel that leads to the igloo. Huskies are very important to Eskimos because they pull their sleds and help with hunting. Eskimos are excellent hunters. Many, many years ago they learned to make **harpoons** and spears to help them hunt their food.

Eskimos get much of their food from the sea, especially fish, seals and whales. Often, an Eskimo will go out in a **kayak** to fish. Only one Eskimo fits inside, and he drives it with a paddle. The waves may turn the kayak upside down, but the Eskimo does not fall out. He is so skillful with a paddle that he quickly is right side up again.

A husky is a large, strong dog.

An Eskimo is a member of the race of people who live on the Arctic coasts of North America and in parts of Greenland.

Igloos are houses made of packed snow.

A kayak is a one-person canoe made of animal skins.

Harpoons are spears with a long rope attached. They are used for spearing whales and other large sea animals.

25

Reading Skills: Context Clues

Directions: In each sentence below, circle the correct meaning for the nonsense word.

1. Be careful when you put that plate back on the shelf—it is **quibbable**.
   flexible colorful (breakable)
2. What is your favorite kind of **tonn**, pears or bananas?
   (fruit) salad purple
3. The **dinlay** outside this morning was very chilly; I needed my sweater.
   tree vegetable (temperature)
4. The whole class enjoyed the **weat**. They wanted to see it again next Friday.
   colorful plant (video)
5. Ashley's mother brought in a **zundy** she made by hand.
   temperature (quilt) plant
6. "Why don't you sit over here, Ronnie? That **sloey** is not very comfortable," said Mr. Gross.
   (chair) car cat

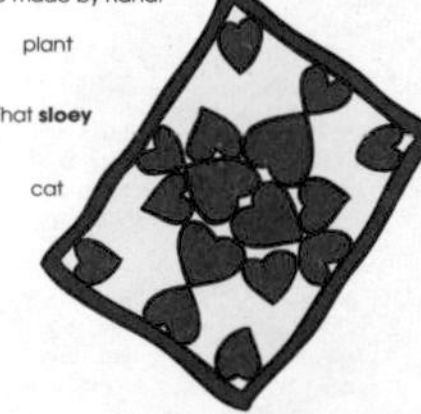

26

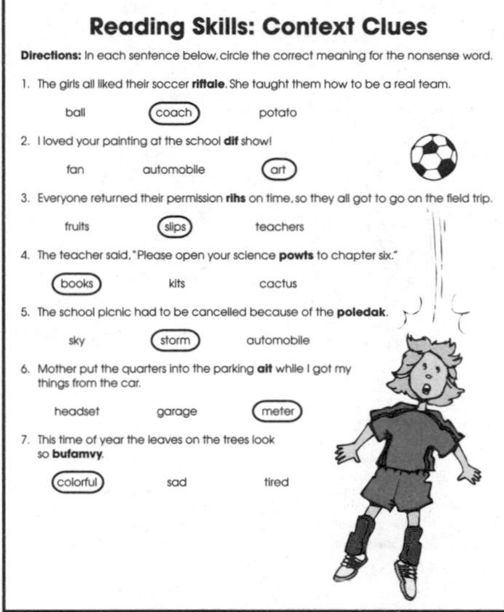

Reading Skills: Context Clues

Directions: In each sentence below, circle the correct meaning for the nonsense word.

1. The girls all liked their soccer **riffale**. She taught them how to be a real team.
   ball (coach) potato
2. I loved your painting at the school **dif** show!
   fan automobile (art)
3. Everyone returned their permission **rihs** on time, so they all got to go on the field trip.
   fruits (slips) teachers
4. The teacher said, "Please open your science **powts** to chapter six."
   (books) kits cactus
5. The school picnic had to be cancelled because of the **poledak**.
   sky (storm) automobile
6. Mother put the quarters into the parking **alt** while I got my things from the car.
   headset garage (meter)
7. This time of year the leaves on the trees look so **bufamvy**.
   (colorful) sad tired

27

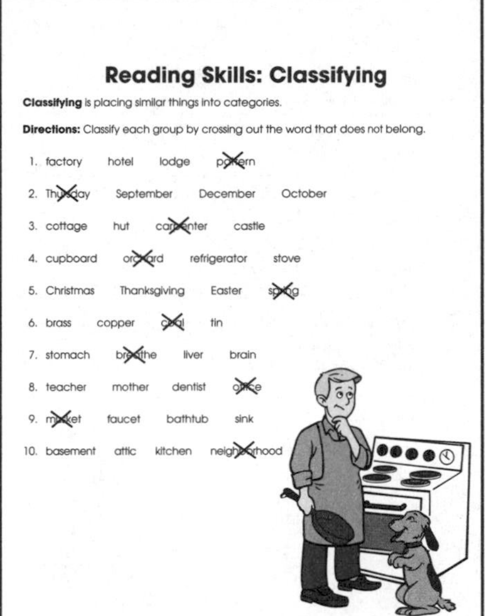

Reading Skills: Classifying

Classifying is placing similar things into categories.

Directions: Classify each group by crossing out the word that does not belong.

1. factory hotel lodge ~~pattern~~
2. ~~Thursday~~ September December October
3. cottage hut ~~carpenter~~ castle
4. cupboard ~~orchard~~ refrigerator stove
5. Christmas Thanksgiving Easter ~~spring~~
6. brass copper ~~coal~~ tin
7. stomach ~~breathe~~ liver brain
8. teacher mother dentist ~~office~~
9. ~~market~~ faucet bathtub sink
10. basement attic kitchen ~~neighborhood~~

28

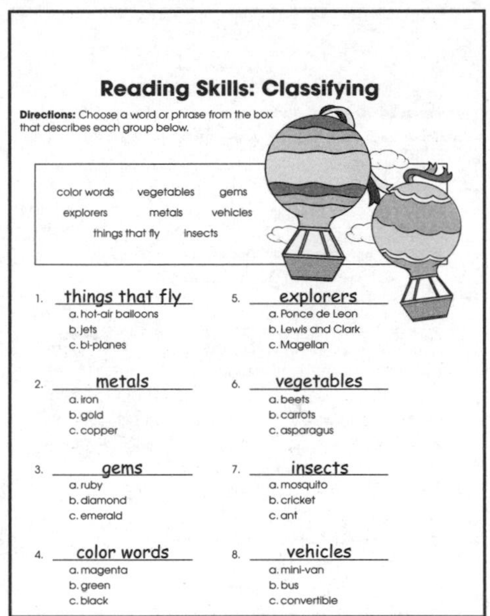

Reading Skills: Classifying

Directions: Choose a word or phrase from the box that describes each group below.

color words	vegetables	gems
explorers	metals	vehicles
things that fly	insects	

1. things that fly
   a. hot-air balloons
   b. jets
   c. bi-planes
2. metals
   a. iron
   b. gold
   c. copper
3. gems
   a. ruby
   b. diamond
   c. emerald
4. color words
   a. magenta
   b. green
   c. black
5. explorers
   a. Ponce de Leon
   b. Lewis and Clark
   c. Magellan
6. vegetables
   a. beets
   b. carrots
   c. asparagus
7. insects
   a. mosquito
   b. cricket
   c. ant
8. vehicles
   a. mini-van
   b. bus
   c. convertible

29

Reading Skills: Classifying

Directions: Read the title of each TV show. Write the correct number to tell what kind of show it is.

1 — Cooking	3 — Sports	5 — Humor
2 — Nature	4 — Mystery	6 — Famous People

4 *The Secret of the Lost Locket*
3 *Learn Tennis With the Pros*
2 *Birds in the Wild*
6 *The Life of George Washington*
1 *Great Recipes From Around the World*
5 *A Laugh a Minute*

Directions: Read the description of each TV show. Write the number of each show above in the blank.

6 The years before he became the first president of the United States are examined.
2 Featured: eagles and owls
4 Clues lead Detective Logan to a cemetery in his search for the missing necklace.
3 Famous players give tips on buying a racket.
1 Six ways to cook chicken
5 Cartoon characters in short stories

30

Reading Skills: Classifying

Directions: Complete each idea by crossing out the word or phrase that does not belong.

1. If the main idea is **things that are green**, I don't need:
   ~~the sun~~ apples grass leaves in summer
2. If the idea is **musical instruments**, I don't need a:
   piano trombone ~~beach ball~~ tuba
3. If the idea is **months of the year**, I don't need:
   ~~Friday~~ January July October
4. If the idea is **colors on the U.S. flag**, I don't need:
   white blue ~~black~~ red
5. If the idea is **types of weather**, I don't need:
   sleet stormy ~~roses~~ sunny
6. If the idea is **fruits**, I don't need:
   kiwi orange ~~spinach~~ banana
7. If the idea is **U.S. presidents**, I don't need:
   Lincoln ~~Jordan~~ Washington Adams
8. If the idea is **flowers**, I don't need:
   ~~oak~~ daisy tulip daffodil
9. If the idea is **sports**, I don't need:
   ~~pears~~ soccer wrestling baseball

31

Reading Skills: Classifying

Directions: Read the Story. Find words in the story that belong in the lists below. Write the words under the correct lists.

Meg, Joey and Ryan are talking about what they want to do when they grow up. Meg says, "I want to be a great writer. I'll write lots of books, and articles for newspapers and magazines."

"I want to be a famous athlete," says Joey. "I'll play baseball in the summer and football in the fall."

"Oh, yes," adds Meg. "I want to be a famous tennis star, too. When I'm not busy writing books, I'll play in tournaments all over the world. I'll be the world's champion!"

Ryan says, "That sounds pretty good. But I think I'll be a doctor and a carpenter. I'll build my very own cabin that I can live in during the winter."

"I'm going to live in a lighthouse by the sea," says Joey. "I've always wanted to do that. Then I can go fishing any time I want."

"I suppose I'll live in a castle when I grow up," says Meg. "World champion tennis players make lots of money!"

Jobs
1. writer
2. athlete
3. doctor
4. carpenter

Sports
1. football
2. baseball
3. tennis
4. fishing

Seasons
1. summer
2. fall
3. winter

Houses
1. cabin
2. lighthouse
3. castle

32

Reading Skills: Analogies

An **analogy** is a way of comparing things to show how they are similar.

Directions: Read the sentences below. Determine how the first pair of words is related. Complete the second pair that relates in the same way. The first one is done for you.

cut	carry	ran	arm	listen
paint	lie	children	50	out
puppy	summer	hot	water	egg

1. Pencil is to write as brush is to paint.
2. Foot is to leg as hand is to arm.
3. Crayons are to draw as scissors are to cut.
4. Leg is to walk as arm is to carry.
5. Baby is to babies as child is to children.
6. Eye is to look as ear is to listen.
7. Chair is to sit as bed is to lie.
8. 600 is to 300 as 100 is to 50.
9. White is to black as in is to out.
10. Ice skate is to winter as swim is to summer.
11. Switch is to light as faucet is to water.
12. Fly is to flew as run is to ran.
13. Cow is to milk as chicken is to egg.
14. Cool is to cold as warm is to hot.
15. Cat is to kitten as dog is to puppy.

33

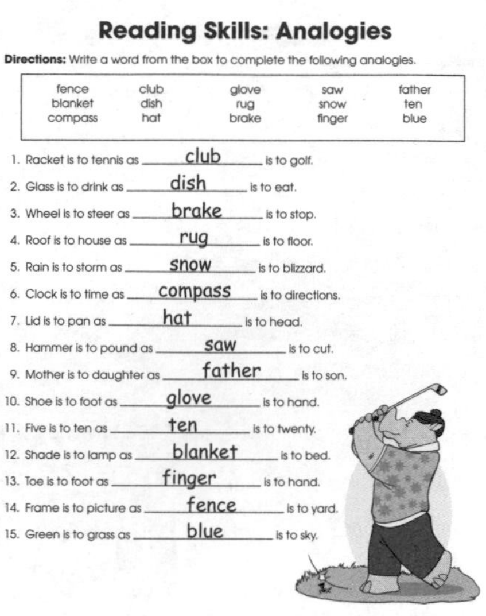

Reading Skills: Analogies

Directions: Write a word from the box to complete the following analogies.

fence	club	glove	saw	father
blanket	dish	rug	snow	ten
compass	hat	brake	finger	blue

1. Racket is to tennis as club is to golf.
2. Glass is to drink as dish is to eat.
3. Wheel is to steer as brake is to stop.
4. Roof is to house as rug is to floor.
5. Rain is to storm as snow is to blizzard.
6. Clock is to time as compass is to directions.
7. Lid is to pan as hat is to head.
8. Hammer is to pound as saw is to cut.
9. Mother is to daughter as father is to son.
10. Shoe is to foot as glove is to hand.
11. Five is to ten as ten is to twenty.
12. Shade is to lamp as blanket is to bed.
13. Toe is to foot as finger is to hand.
14. Frame is to picture as fence is to yard.
15. Green is to grass as blue is to sky.

34

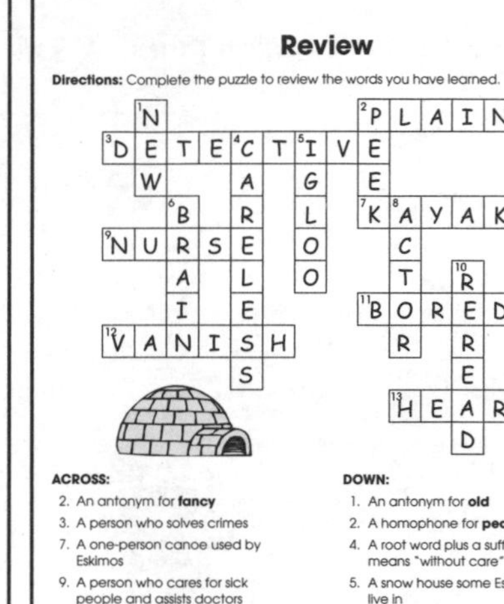

Review

Directions: Complete the puzzle to review the words you have learned.

ACROSS:

2. An antonym for **fancy**
3. A person who solves crimes
7. A one-person canoe used by Eskimos
9. A person who cares for sick people and assists doctors
11. A homophone for **board**
12. A synonym for **disappear**
13. This pumps blood with every beat

DOWN:

1. An antonym for **old**
2. A homophone for **peak**
4. A root word plus a suffix that means "without care"
5. A snow house some Eskimos live in
6. You think with this
8. A person who performs in a movie or play
10. A prefix plus a root word that means "read again"

35

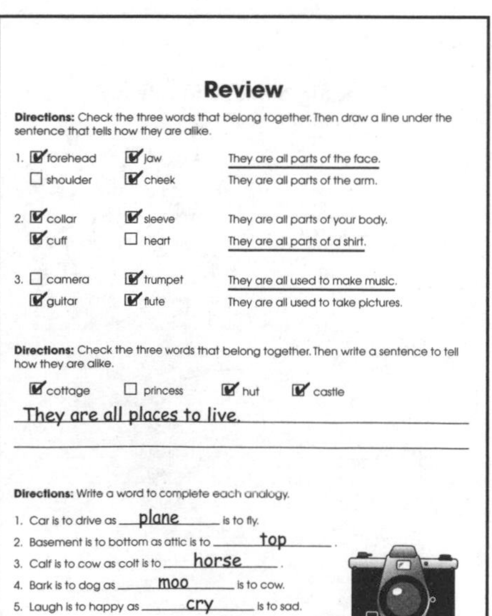

Review

Directions: Check the three words that belong together. Then draw a line under the sentence that tells how they are alike.

1. ☑ forehead ☑ jaw ☐ shoulder ☑ cheek — They are all parts of the face. (underlined) / They are all parts of the arm.
2. ☑ collar ☑ sleeve ☑ cuff ☐ heart — They are all parts of your body. / They are all parts of a shirt. (underlined)
3. ☐ camera ☑ trumpet ☑ guitar ☑ flute — They are all used to make music. (underlined) / They are all used to take pictures.

Directions: Check the three words that belong together. Then write a sentence to tell how they are alike.

☑ cottage ☐ princess ☑ hut ☑ castle

They are all places to live.

Directions: Write a word to complete each analogy.

1. Car is to drive as plane is to fly.
2. Basement is to bottom as attic is to top.
3. Calf is to cow as colt is to horse.
4. Bark is to dog as moo is to cow.
5. Laugh is to happy as cry is to sad.

36

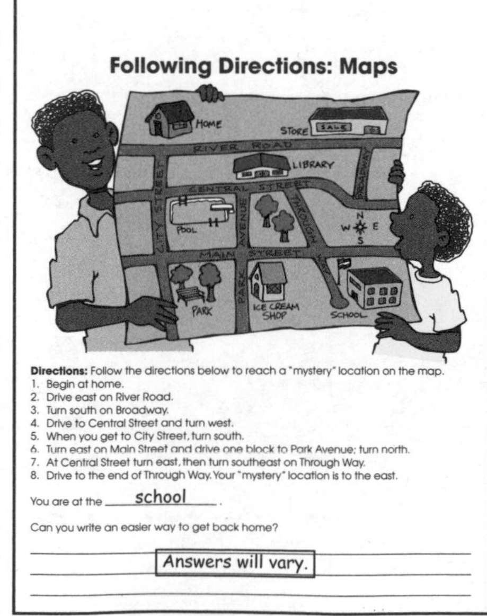

Following Directions: Maps

Directions: Follow the directions below to reach a "mystery" location on the map.

1. Begin at home.
2. Drive east on River Road.
3. Turn south on Broadway.
4. Drive to Central Street and turn west.
5. When you get to City Street, turn south.
6. Turn east on Main Street and drive one block to Park Avenue; turn north.
7. At Central Street turn east, then turn southeast on Through Way.
8. Drive to the end of Through Way. Your "mystery" location is to the east.

You are at the school.

Can you write an easier way to get back home?

Answers will vary.

37

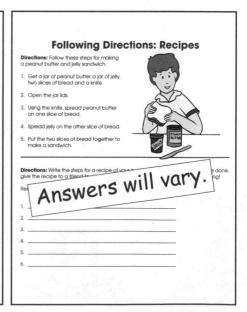

Following Directions: Recipes

Directions: Follow these steps for making a peanut butter and jelly sandwich.

1. Get a jar of peanut butter, a jar of jelly, two slices of bread and a knife.
2. Open the jar lids.
3. Using the knife, spread peanut butter on one slice of bread.
4. Spread jelly on the other slice of bread.
5. Put the two slices of bread together to make a sandwich.

JELLY PEANUT BUTTER

Directions: Write the steps for a recipe of your … done, give the recipe to a friend t… ng!

Re…

Answers will vary.

1.
2.
3.
4.
5.
6.

38

Following Directions: Recipes

Sequencing is putting items or events in logical order.

Directions: Read the recipe. Then number the steps in order for making brownies.

Preheat the oven to 350 degrees. Grease an 8-inch square baking dish.

In a mixing bowl, place two squares (2 ounces) of unsweetened chocolate and 1/3 cup butter. Place the bowl in a pan of hot water and heat it to melt the chocolate and the butter.

When the chocolate is melted, remove the pan from the heat. Add 1 cup sugar and two eggs to the melted chocolate and beat it. Next, stir in 3/4 cup sifted flour, 1/2 teaspoon baking powder and 1/2 teaspoon salt. Finally, mix in 1/2 cup chopped nuts.

Spread the mixture in the greased baking dish. Bake for 30 to 35 minutes. The brownies are done when a toothpick stuck in the center comes out clean. Let the brownies cool. Cut them into squares.

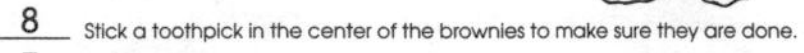

8 Stick a toothpick in the center of the brownies to make sure they are done.
5 Mix in chopped nuts.
2 Melt chocolate and butter in a mixing bowl over a pan of hot water.
9 Cool brownies and cut into squares.
3 Beat in sugar and eggs.
6 Spread mixture in a baking dish.
4 Stir in flour, baking powder and salt.
7 Bake for 30 to 35 minutes.
1 Turn oven to 350 degrees and grease pan.

39

Following Directions: Salt Into Pepper

Directions: Read how to do a magic trick that will amaze your friends. Then number the steps in order to do the trick.

Imagine doing this trick for your friends. Pick up a salt shaker that everyone can see is full of salt. Pour some into your hand. Tell your audience that you will change the salt into pepper. Say a few magic words, such as "Fibbiddy, dibbiddy, milkshake and malt. What will be pepper once was salt!" Then open your hand and pour out pepper!

How is it done? First you need a clear salt shaker with a screw-on top. You also need a paper napkin and a small amount of pepper.

Take off the top of the salt shaker. Lay the napkin over the opening and push it down a little to make a small pocket. Fill the pocket with pepper. Put the top back on the salt shaker and tear off the extra napkin. Now you are ready for the trick.

Hold up the salt shaker so your audience can see that it is full of salt. Shake some "salt" into your hand. Close your fist so no one can see that it is really pepper. Say the magic words and open your hand.

9 Say some magic words.
1 Find a clear salt shaker with a screw-on top.
10 Open your hand and pour out the pepper.
3 Take off the top of the salt shaker.
7 Show the audience the shaker full of salt.
4 Place the napkin over the opening of the salt shaker.
2 Get a paper napkin and some pepper.
5 Put the pepper in the napkin pocket.
8 Shake some "salt" into your hand and close your fist.
6 Put the top back on the salt shaker and tear off the extra napkin.

40

Following Directions: A Rocket Launcher

Directions: Read about how to make a rocket launcher. Then number the steps in order below. **Have an adult help you.**

Here's a science experiment that you can do in your own backyard. To make this rocket launcher, you need an empty 1-quart soda bottle, cork, paper towel, 1/2 cup water, 1/2 cup vinegar and 1 teaspoon baking soda. You may want to add some streamers.

The cork will be the rocket. If you attach tissue paper streamers to the cork with a thumbtack, you will be able to follow the rocket more easily during its flight.

Pour the water and vinegar into the launcher—the bottle. Cut the paper towel into a 4-inch square. Place the baking soda in the middle of the paper towel. Roll up the towel and twist the ends so the baking soda will stay inside.

Outside, where there will be plenty of room for the rocket to fly, drop the paper towel and baking soda into the bottle. Put the cork on as tightly as you can.

The liquid will soak through the paper towel. This lets the baking soda and vinegar work together to make a kind of gas called carbon dioxide. As the carbon dioxide builds up in the bottle, it will push out the cork. Soon the cork will shoot up into the sky with a loud pop!

3 Pour the vinegar and water into the soda bottle.
2 Attach streamers to the cork so you can follow its flight.
8 Stand back and watch your rocket blast off!
4 Place the baking soda on the paper towel and roll it up.
7 Wait as the vinegar and baking soda work to make carbon dioxide gas.
5 Drop the paper towel with the baking soda into the bottle.
1 Gather together a bottle, cork, water, vinegar, paper towel and baking soda.
6 Put on the cork as tightly as you can.

41

Reading Skills: Sequencing

Directions: Read each set of events. Then number them in the correct order.

2 Get dressed for school and hurry downstairs for breakfast.
1 Roll over, sleepy-eyed, and turn off the alarm clock.
3 Meet your friends at the corner to walk to school.

3 The fourth-grade class walked quietly to a safe area away from the building.
2 The teacher reminded the last student to shut the classroom door.
1 The loud clanging of the fire alarm startled everyone in the room.

1 Barb's dad watched from the seat of the tractor as the boys and girls climbed into the wagon.
3 By the time they returned to the barn, there wasn't much straw left.
2 As the wagon bumped along the trail, the boys and girls sang songs they learned in music class.

3 The referee blew his whistle and held up the hand of the winner of the match.
2 Each wrestler worked hard, trying to out-maneuver his opponent.
1 The referee said, "Shake hands, boys, and wrestle a fair match."

42

Reading Skills: Sequencing

Directions: In each group below, one event in the sequence is missing. Write the correct sentence from the box where it belongs.

- Paul put his bait on the hook and cast out into the pond.
- "Sorry," he said, "but the TV repairman can't get here until Friday."
- Everyone pitched in and helped.
- Corey put the ladder up against the trunk of the tree.

1. "All the housework has to be done before anyone goes to the game," said Mom.
2. Everyone pitched in and helped.
3. We all agreed that "many hands make light work."

1. Paul put his bait on the hook and cast out into the pond.
2. It wasn't long until he felt a tug on the line, and we watched the bobber go under.
3. He was the only one to go home with something other than bait!

1. The little girl cried as she stood looking up into the maple tree.
2. Between her tears, she managed to say, "My kitten is up in the tree and can't get down."
3. Corey put the ladder up against the trunk of the tree.

1. Dad hung up the phone and turned to look at us.
2. "Sorry," he said, "but the TV repairman can't get here until Friday."
3. "This would be a good time to get out those old board games in the hall closet," he said.

43

Reading Skills: Sequencing

Directions: In each group below, one event in the sequence is missing. Write a sentence that makes sense in the sequence.

1. The traffic light turned red.
2. __________
3. The police arrived to investigate.

1. __________
2. __________
3. N... ew clothes.

Answers will vary.

1. The weatherman said that we could expect a heavy snowfall during the night.
2. When Dad got home from work, he told us the roads were getting very slippery.
3. __________

1. Mom opened the kitchen drawer and reached in.
2. __________
3. "Jody, please go get a bandage for me from the bathroom," she said.

44

Reading Skills: Sequencing

Directions: In each group below, one event in the sequence is missing. Write a sentence that makes sense in the sequence.

1. The clouds grew very dark and we could hear thunder.
2. All of a sudden, the wind started to blow very hard.
3. _____

1. The volleyball game was very boring at first.
2. _____
3. The [illegible]

1. _____
2. The boys gathered all the garden tools and put them in the wheelbarrow.
3. "Well, it was hard work, but we got it done, boys!" said Jim.

1. The teacher gave us our homework assignment early in the day.
2. Since the school assembly had to be cancelled, we had an extra study hall.
3. _____

1. Our cat has been acting very strange lately.
2. We heard unusual noises coming from the hall closet.
3. _____

Answers will vary.

45

Reading Skills: Sequencing

Directions: Reread the story, if necessary. Then choose an important event from the beginning, middle and end of the story, and write it below.

Beginning: _____

Middle: _____

End: _____

Answers will vary.

Directions: Number these story events in the order in which they happened.

4 Jonny's mom called the doctor to get an appointment since Jonny's ankle was red and swollen.
1 Jonny limped to the top of the stairs.
6 The pediatrician thought Jonny might have JRA.
3 The sitter told Jonny's mom that he had slept most of the day.
5 The doctor gave them a prescription for an antibiotic.
7 Jonny is now 29 years old.
2 Jonny told his mom, "My leg hurts."

48

Reading Skills: Recalling Details

Directions: Answer the questions below about "Jonny's Story."

1. How old was Jonny when his ankle began to bother him? 3 1/2 years
2. Why did Jonny's mom stay home from work the second day? Because Jonny was feeling worse.
3. What do the letters JRA stand for? juvenile rheumatoid arthritis
4. When Jonny and his mom were waiting to see the doctor, how did Jonny's mom know he must not be feeling well? Because he slept the whole time.
5. Where did Jonny's mom take him when she picked him up at the sitter's house? to the doctor's office.

Directions: Write the letter of the definition beside the word it defines. If you need help, use a dictionary or check the context of the story.

a. strong medicine used to treat infections
b. found to be true
c. doctor that specializes in child care
d. not yet an adult
e. did not walk correctly

C pediatrician
A antibiotic
B confirmed
E limped
D juvenile

49

Reading Skills: Sequencing

Directions: Reread the story, if necessary. Then choose an important event from the beginning, middle and end of the story, and write it below.

Beginning: _____

Middle: _____

End: _____

Answers will vary.

Directions: Number these story events in the order in which they happened.

4 Paul moaned, "Oh, no! I left my lunch on the table at home!"
1 Megan watched as the bus stopped at Emily's house to pick up Emily and her little sister.
5 Miss Haynes sent Paul to the cafeteria with a note explaining the problem.
3 The teacher said they had some business to take care of before they could leave on the trip.
6 Paul quickly returned with a sack lunch packed by the cafeteria helpers.
2 Megan told Emily, "I see you remembered your sack lunch."
7 The fourth graders finally loaded onto the bus for the field trip.

52

Reading Skills: Recalling Details

Directions: Answer the questions below about "Class Field Trip."

1. Who were the two adult helpers that would be going on the trip with Miss Haynes' class? Ms. Diehl and Mrs. Denes
2. The students in Miss Haynes' class were excited about the field trip for different reasons. What were the three different reasons mentioned in the story?
   a. They got to ride the bus.
   b. They enjoyed learning about their town's history.
   c. They got a day out of school.
3. What business did Miss Haynes need to take care of before the class could leave on its trip? Check attendance and pass out name tags.

Directions: Write the letter of the definition beside the word it defines. If you need help, use a dictionary or check the context of the story.

a. sat down, not very gently
b. easy to understand; without doubt
c. family members that lived in the past, such as grandparents
d. in a favorable way

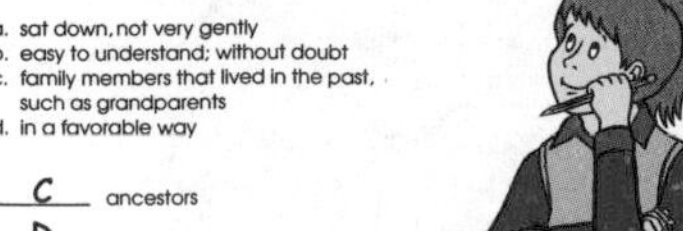

C ancestors
D fortunately
A plopped
B obviously

53

Reading Skills: Sequencing

Directions: Read about how a tadpole becomes a frog. Then number the stages in order below.

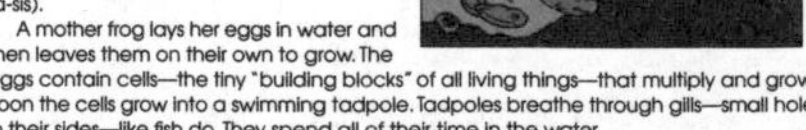

Frogs and toads belong to a group of animals called amphibians (am-FIB-ee-ans). This means "living a double life." Frogs and toads live a "double life" because they live part of their lives in water and part on land. They are able to do this because their bodies change as they grow. This series of changes is called metamorphosis (met-a-MORE-fa-sis).

A mother frog lays her eggs in water and then leaves them on their own to grow. The eggs contain cells—the tiny "building blocks" of all living things—that multiply and grow. Soon the cells grow into a swimming tadpole. Tadpoles breathe through gills—small holes in their sides—like fish do. They spend all of their time in the water.

The tadpole changes as it grows. Back legs slowly form. Front legs begin inside the tadpole under the gill holes. They pop out when they are fully developed. At the same time, lungs, which a frog uses to breathe instead of gills, are almost ready to be used.

As the tadpole reaches the last days of its life in the water, its tail seems to disappear. When all of the tadpole's body parts are ready for life on land, it has become a frog.

6 The front legs pop out. The lungs are ready to use for breathing.
2 The cells in the egg multiply and grow.
8 The tadpole has become a frog.
4 Back legs slowly form.
3 Soon the cells grow into a swimming tadpole.
5 Front legs develop inside the tadpole.
7 The tadpole's tail seems to disappear.
1 A mother frog lays her eggs in water.

54

Reading Skills: Main Idea in Sentences

The **main idea** is the most important idea, or main point, in a sentence, paragraph or story.

Directions: Circle the main idea for each sentence.

1. Emily knew she would be late if she watched the end of the TV show.
   a. Emily likes watching TV.
   b. Emily is always running late.
   (c.) If Emily didn't leave, she would be late.
2. The dog was too strong and pulled Jason across the park on his leash.
   (a.) The dog is stronger than Jason.
   b. Jason is not very strong.
   c. Jason took the dog for a walk.
3. Jennifer took the book home so she could read it over and over.
   a. Jennifer loves to read.
   (b.) Jennifer loves the book.
   c. Jennifer is a good reader.
4. Jerome threw the baseball so hard it broke the window.
   (a.) Jerome throws baseballs very hard.
   b. Jerome was mad at the window.
   c. Jerome can't throw very straight.
5. Lori came home and decided to clean the kitchen for her parents.
   a. Lori is a very nice person.
   (b.) Lori did a favor for her parents.
   c. Lori likes to cook.
6. It was raining so hard that it was hard to see the road through the windshield.
   a. It always rains hard in April.
   (b.) The rain blurred our vision.
   c. It's hard to drive in the rain.

55

Reading Skills: Main Idea in Paragraphs

Directions: Read each paragraph below. Then circle the sentence that tells the main idea.

It looked as if our class field day would have to be cancelled due to the weather. We tried not to show our disappointment, but Mr. Wade knew that it was hard to keep our minds on the math lesson. We noticed that even he had been sneaking glances out the window. All morning the classroom had been buzzing with plans. Each team met to plan team strategies for winning the events. Then, it happened! Clouds began to cover the sky, and soon the thunder and lightning confirmed what we were afraid of—field day cancelled. Mr. Wade explained that we could still keep our same teams. We could put all of our plans into motion, but we would have to get busy and come up with some inside games and competitions. I guess the day would not be a total disaster!

a. Many storms occur in the late afternoon.

(b.) Our class field day had to be cancelled due to the weather.

c. Each team came up with its own strategies.

Allison and Emma had to work quietly and quickly to get Mom's birthday cake baked before she got home from work. Each of the girls had certain jobs to do—Allison set the oven temperature and got the cake pans prepared, while Emma got out all the ingredients. As they stirred and mixed, the two girls talked about the surprise party Dad had planned for Mom. Even Dad didn't know that the girls were baking this special cake. The cake was delicious. "It shows you what teamwork can do!" said the girls in unison.

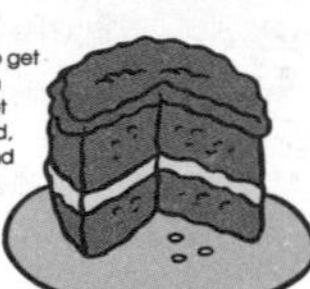

a. Dad worked with the girls to bake the cake.

b. Mom's favorite frosting is chocolate cream.

(c.) Allison and Emma baked a birthday cake for Mom.

56

Reading Skills: Main Idea in Paragraphs

Directions: Read each paragraph below. Then circle the sentence that tells the main idea.

During the summer, Lori got a job at the city animal shelter. She loved petting the kittens and hearing them purr. She loved washing the dogs and watching them run around the yard. It was always fun and exciting to watch new animals come in, but it was even better watching animals get new homes with good families. When the city threatened to close the shelter due to money problems, Lori worked hard at a special car wash, bake sale and other fund-raisers to raise money. Luckily, they kept the shelter open! Lori said she would continue working even when school started, because she felt she was doing something worthwhile to help her community.

a. The animal shelter was almost closed by the city.

(b.) Lori loved working at the animal shelter.

c. Lori loved petting the animals.

Gary worked as a lifeguard last summer at the resort. One afternoon, a young girl and her mother came to the poolside to play. While the girl's mother went to get some iced tea, the little girl ran around the pool, playing with her new toys. Gary watched carefully and told the girl not to run, but she was too busy playing to pay attention. Just as Gary was climbing off the lifeguard stand to stop the girl from hurting herself, she slipped and fell into the deep end of the pool. Gary jumped in after her just in time. She didn't know how to swim. Just as Gary was lifting the girl from the water, her mother ran back to the pool. The girl was fine, but Gary warned her mother never to leave her daughter unattended by the pool, not even for a minute. The little girl was fine, and her mother was forever grateful for Gary's watchful eyes.

a. Young children should never be left unattended by the pool.

b. Being a lifeguard can be rewarding.

(c.) Gary saved a little girl from drowning last summer.

57

Reading Skills: Main Idea in Poetry

Directions: Read the verse from this poem written by Lord Tennyson, "The Charge of the Light Brigade." Then answer the questions below.

"Forward the Light Brigade!"

Was there a man dismayed?
Not though the soldier knew
  Someone had blundered.
Theirs not to make reply,
Theirs not to reason why,
Theirs but to do and die.
Into the valley of Death
  Rode the six hundred.

1. Circle the main idea:

   Soldiers in battle always fight in groups of 600.

   (Soldiers in battle must follow orders without question.)

2. What word in the verse means "made a mistake"? blundered
3. What two things must a soldier not do?
   a. make reply
   b. reason why
4. What does Tennyson say is the responsibility of a soldier?
   to do and die

58

Reading Skills: Fact and Opinion

A **fact** is a statement that can be proven true. An **opinion** is a statement that tells how someone feels or what he/she thinks about something or someone.

Example:
Fact: Ms. Davis is the new principal at Hayes Elementary.
Opinion: Ms. Davis is the nicest principal we ever had.

Directions: Read each pair of sentences below. One is a fact; one is an opinion. Write **F** before the fact and **O** before the opinion.

O 1. Soccer is the best sport at our school.
F More students at our school play soccer than any other sport.
F 2. Grandmother Hall lives in Clarksburg.
O Grandmother Hall makes the best chocolate-chip cookies!
F 3. The county fair gate opens at 10:00 a.m.
O We're going to have a great time at the fair.
O 4. The drive along the river is very scenic.
F It is a 5-mile drive along the river.
O 5. Computers make our work much easier.
F We have four computers in our classroom.
O 6. *The Cinnamon Lake Mysteries* is a very good series.
F Our library has several copies of *The Cinnamon Lake Mysteries*.
F 7. Jerry falls asleep in class every day!
O Jerry is so tired, he can't stay awake.
O 8. That car is too old to make it across the country.
F That car was built in 1964.

59

Fact and Opinion

Directions: Write **F** before the facts and **O** before the opinions.

F 1. Our school football team has a winning season this year.
O 2. Mom's spaghetti is the best in the world!
O 3. Autumn is the nicest season of the year.
F 4. Mrs. Burns took her class on a field trip last Thursday.
F 5. The library always puts 30 books in our classroom book collection.
O 6. They should put only books about horses in the collection.
O 7. Our new art teacher is very strict.
O 8. Everyone should keep take-home papers in a folder so they don't have to look for them when it is time to go home.
F 9. The bus to the mall goes right by her house at 7:45 a.m.
O 10. Our new superintendent, Mr. Willeke, is very nice.

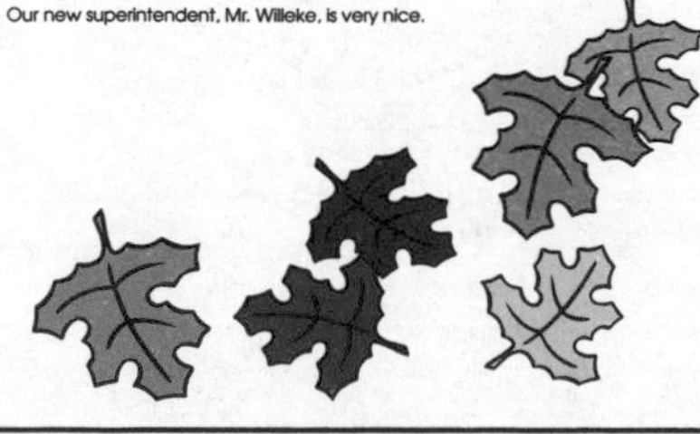

60

Fact and Opinion

Directions: Each fact sentence below has a "partner" opinion sentence in the box. Match "partners" by writing the correct sentences on the lines.

Maps can be very difficult to figure out.	Those brownies tasted awful!
The bridesmaids' dresses turned out beautiful!	Each child in here needs a computer.
You make the best cherry pie.	She is the best artist in the class.
If I can't go to the party, I will be really upset.	That car is so old, it looks like it will fall apart.

1. Paige helped her mother bake brownies last night.
   Those brownies tasted awful!
2. Katherine made all the drawings for the book.
   She is the best artist in the class.
3. That cherry tree is full of cherries.
   You make the best cherry pie.
4. We have four computers in the classroom.
   Each child in here needs a computer.
5. Mom made dresses for all of my bridesmaids.
   The bridesmaids' dresses turned out beautiful!
6. If I can't go to the party, I won't be able to give her the present.
   If I can't go to the party, I will be really upset.
7. The car is old and rusty.
   That car is so old, it looks like it will fall apart.
8. However he looked at it, he still couldn't figure out the map.
   Maps can be very difficult to figure out.

61

Review

Directions: Read the paragraph. Then circle the sentence that tells the main idea.

Justin and Mina did everything together. They rode their bikes to school together, ate their lunches together, did their homework together, and even spent their weekends together playing baseball and video games. Even though Justin and Mina sometimes argued about silly things, they still loved being together. Sometimes the arguments were even fun, because then they got to make up! People often thought they were brother and sister because they sounded alike and even looked alike! Justin and Mina promised they would be friends forever.

(a.) Justin and Mina did everything together.

b. Justin and Mina like riding bikes.

c. Justin and Mina like to argue.

Directions: Write **F** before the facts and **O** before the opinions.

O 1. Justin loved to ride his bike.
F 2. Mina promised they would always be friends.
O 3. Justin and Mina should never argue.
O 4. Justin's dog needed to be washed.
F 5. That car is only big enough for three people!
F 6. The laundry basket is in the corner of the basement.
O 7. That laundry needs to be done today.
O 8. Brownies are my favorite snack.
F 9. She made chocolate cake for Mom's birthday.
F 10. I came all the way from Texas to see you.

62

Reading Comprehension: Your Five Senses

Your senses are very important to you. You depend on them every day. They tell you where you are and what is going on around you. Your senses are sight, hearing, touch, smell and taste.

Try to imagine for a minute that you were suddenly unable to use your senses. Imagine, for instance, that you are in a cave and your only source of light is a candle. Without warning, a gust of wind blows out the flame.

Your senses are always at work. Your eyes let you read this book. Your nose brings the scent of dinner cooking. Your hand feels the softness as you stroke a puppy. Your ears tell you that a storm is approaching.

Your senses also help keep you from harm. They warn you if you touch something that will burn you. They keep you from looking at a light that is too bright, and they tell you if a car is coming up behind you. Each of your senses collects information and sends it as a message to your brain. The brain is like the control center for your body. It sorts out the messages sent by your senses and acts on them.

Directions: Answer these questions about the five senses.

1. Circle the main idea:
   Your senses keep you from harm.
   (Your senses are important to you in many ways.)
2. Name the five senses.
   a. sight
   b. hearing
   c. touch
   d. smell
   e. taste
3. Which part of your body acts as the "control center"?
   your brain

63

Reading Comprehension: Touch

Unlike the other senses, which are located only in your head, your sense of touch is all over your body. Throughout your life, you receive an endless flow of information about the world and yourself from your sense of touch. It tells you if something is hot or cold, hard or soft. It sends messages of pain, such as a headache or sore throat, if there is a problem.

There are thousands of tiny sensors all over your body. They are all linked together. These sensors are also linked to your spinal cord and your brain to make up your central nervous system. Through this system, the various parts of your body can send messages to your brain. It is then the brain's job to decide what it is you are actually feeling. All this happens in just a split second.

Not all parts of your body have the same amount of feeling. Areas that have the most nerves, or sensors, have the greatest amount of feeling. For instance, the tips of your fingers have more feeling than parts of your arm.

Some sensors get used to the feeling of an object after a period of time. When you first put your shirt on in the morning, you can feel its pressure on your skin. However, some of the sensors stop responding during the day.

One feeling you cannot get used to is the feeling of pain. Pain is an important message, because it tells your brain that something harmful is happening to you. Your brain reacts by doing something right away to protect you.

Directions: Answer these questions about the sense of touch.

1. Circle the main idea:
   (The sense of touch is all over your body.)
   You cannot get used to the sense of pain.
2. The nerves, spinal cord and brain are linked together to make the central nervous system.
3. One feeling you can never get used to is pain.
4. All parts of your body have the same amount of feeling. True (False)
5. It is the brain's job to receive messages from the sensors on your body and decide what you are actually feeling. (True) False

64

Reading Comprehension: Smell

Your nose is your sense organ for smelling. Smells are mixed into the air around you. They enter your nose when you breathe.

In the upper part of your nose, there are special smell sensors. They pick up smells and send messages to your brain. The brain then decides what it is you are smelling.

Smelling can be a pleasant sense. Sometimes smells can remind you of a person or place. For instance, have you ever smelled a particular scent and then suddenly thought about your grandmother's house? Smell also can make you feel hungry. In fact, your sense of smell is linked very closely to your sense of taste. Without your sense of smell, you would not taste food as strongly.

Smelling also can be quite unpleasant. But this, too, is important. By smelling food you can tell if it is spoiled and not fit to eat. Your sense of smell also can sometimes warn you of danger, such as a fire.

The sense of smell tires out more quickly than your other senses. This is why you get used to some everyday smells and no longer notice them after a while.

Directions: Answer these questions about the sense of smell.

1. Smells are mixed in the air around you.
2. The sense of smell is linked closely to the sense of taste.
3. Give an example of why smelling bad smells can be important to you.
   You can smell spoiled food or be warned of danger like a fire.

65

Reading Comprehension: Taste

The senses of taste and smell work very closely together. If you can't smell your food, it is difficult to recognize the taste. You may have noticed this when you've had a bad cold with a stuffed-up nose.

Tasting is the work of your tongue. All over your tongue are tiny taste sensors called taste buds. If you look at your tongue in a mirror, you can see small groups of taste buds. They are what give your tongue its rough appearance. Each taste bud has a small opening in it. Tiny pieces of food and drink enter this opening. There taste sensors gather information about the taste and send messages to your brain. Your brain decides what the taste is.

Taste buds located in different areas of your tongue recognize different tastes. There are only four tastes your tongue can recognize: sweet, sour, bitter and salty. All other flavors are a mixture of taste and smell.

Directions: Answer these questions about the sense of taste.

1. It is difficult to taste your food if you can't smell.
2. The tiny taste sensors on your tongue are called taste buds.
3. The four tastes that your tongue can recognize are sweet, sour, bitter and salty.
4. All other flavors are a mixture of taste and smell.

66

Reading Comprehension: Sight

You can see this page because of light. Without light, there would be no sight. In a dark room, you might see only a a few large shapes. If it is pitch black, you can't see anything at all.

Light reflects or bounces off things and then travels to your eyes. The light enters your eye through the pupil. The pupil is the black circle in the middle of your eye. It gets bigger in low light to let in as much light as possible. In bright light, it shrinks so that too much light doesn't get in.

Light enters through the pupil and then passes through the lens. The lens bends the light so that it falls on the back of your eye on the retina. The retina has millions of tiny cells that are very sensitive to light. When an image is formed in the eye, it is upside down. This image is sent to your brain. The brain receives the message and turns the picture right side up again.

Some people are far-sighted. This means they can clearly see things that are far away, but things close by may be blurred. People who are near-sighted can clearly see things better if they are close by. Glasses or contact lenses can help correct these problems.

Some people can see only a little bit or perhaps not at all. This is called being blind. Blind people rely on their sense of touch to learn more about the world. They can even use their sense of touch to read. Some blind people read with a special printing system called Braille. The system is named for the man who invented it. Braille has small raised dots instead of letters on a page.

Directions: Answer these questions about the sense of sight.

1. Without light, there would be no sight.
2. Reflect means to bounce off of.
3. The part of the eye that controls the amount of light entering your eye by getting bigger and smaller is called the pupil.
4. To correct near-sightedness or far-sightedness, you can wear glasses or contact lenses.
5. What is the name of the special printing system for blind people? Braille

67

Reading Comprehension: Hearing

Every sound you hear is made by the movement of air. These movements, called vibrations, spread out in waves. Your outer ear collects these "sound waves" and sends them down a tube to the inner ear. The vibrations hit the eardrum, a flap of skin stretched across the inner end of the tube. As the eardrum vibrates, a tiny bone called the hammer moves back and forth. This helps the vibrations move to three small bones and then to the cochlea, where they are changed to nerve impulses. The impulses travel to the brain where they are recognized as sounds.

Some people have trouble hearing or cannot hear at all. This is called being deaf. Some deaf people can understand what you are saying by watching how your lips move. They use their eyes as their ears. Sometimes a hearing aid can help improve hearing. It is like a tiny radio that fits into the ear. Sounds enter the hearing aid and are made much louder.

Deaf people also have difficulty learning to speak because they cannot hear how to say words. Many deaf people "talk" by making pictures with their hands. This kind of talking is called sign language. Every letter of the alphabet has a sign. These signs are shown above.

a b c d e f g h i j k l m n o p q r s t u v w x y z

Directions: Answer these questions about the sense of hearing.

1. Sound is made by movements of the air called vibrations.
2. The flap of skin stretched over the inner end of the tube inside your ear is called the eardrum.
3. People who cannot hear are said to be deaf.
4. The language of making pictures with your hands is called sign language.
5. Read this word in sign language.
   It says hear.

68

Reading Comprehension: The Five Senses

Directions: Before each sentence, write the sense—hearing, sight, smell, taste or touch—that is being used. The first one is done for you.

hearing 1. The rooster crows outside my window early each morning.
touch 2. After playing in the snow, our fingers and toes were freezing.
hearing 3. I could hear sirens in the distance.
sight 4. I think this tree is taller than that one.
taste 5. The delicious salad was filled with fresh, juicy fruits.
smell 6. The odor of the bread baking in the oven was wonderful.
sight 7. There was a rainbow in the sky today.
touch 8. The kitten was soft and fluffy.
smell 9. Her perfume filled the air when she walked by.
sight 10. An airplane wrote a message in the sky.
taste 11. The chocolate cake was yummy.
hearing 12. The steamboat whistle frightened the baby.
taste 13. The sour lemon made my lips pucker.
hearing 14. Her gum-popping got on my nerves.

69

Reading Comprehension: The Five Senses

Directions: Each word in the word box makes you think of hearing, sight, smell, taste or touch. Write each word under the sense that is used. One is done for you.

~~music~~	~~rainbow~~	~~talking~~	~~hot~~	~~sour~~
~~honking~~	~~moldy~~	~~butterfly~~	~~green~~	~~book~~
~~crying~~	~~silky~~	~~sweet~~	~~smoky~~	~~bitter~~
~~salty~~	~~skunk~~	~~cold~~	~~smooth~~	~~stinky~~

Touch	Sight	Taste
silky	rainbow	salty
cold	butterfly	sweet
hot	green	sour
smooth	book	bitter

Smell	Hearing
skunk	music
smoky	honking
stinky	talking
moldy	crying

70

Reading Comprehension: Helen Keller

A B C D E F G H I J K L M
N O P Q R S T U V W X Y Z

The story of Helen Keller has given courage and hope to many people. Helen had many problems, but she used her life to do great things.

When Helen Keller was a child, she often behaved in a wild way. She was very bright and strong, but she could not tell people what she was thinking or feeling. And she didn't know how others thought or felt. Helen was blind and deaf.

Helen was born with normal hearing and sight, but this changed when she was 1 year old. She had a serious illness with a very high fever. After that, Helen was never able to see or hear again.

As a child, Helen was angry and lonely. But when she was 6 years old, her parents got a teacher for her. They brought a young woman named Anne Sullivan to stay at their house and help Helen. After much hard work, Helen began to learn sign language. Anne taught Helen many important things, such as how to behave like other children. Because Helen was so smart, she learned things very quickly. She learned how to read Braille. By the time she was 8 years old, she was becoming very famous. People were amazed at what she could do.

Helen continued to learn. She even learned how to speak. When she was 20 years old, she went to college. Helen did so well in college that a magazine paid her to write the story of her life. After college, she earned money by writing and giving speeches. She traveled all around the world. She worked to get special schools and libraries for the blind and deaf. She wrote many books, including one about her teacher, Anne Sullivan.

Here is how "Helen" is written in Braille:

Directions: Answer these questions about Helen Keller.

1. What caused Helen to be blind and deaf? She had a very serious illness with a high fever.
2. What happy thing happened when Helen was 6 years old? Her parents got her a special teacher.
3. What was her teacher's name? Anne Sullivan

71

Review

In this book, you have learned new ways to write and "talk." There are many other ways to express your thoughts to others. Here is another one.

For hundreds of years, Native Americans used their own system of sign language. These signs were understood by all tribes, even though their spoken languages were different.

The Plains tribes helped to develop and spread sign language. The Plains tribes liked to wander. They never camped in any one place for long. They used sign language so they could talk with other Native Americans wherever they went.

The first white adventurers and trappers in America also learned Native American sign language. They wanted to understand and be understood by the Native Americans.

Many Native Americans today still use this ancient form of talking. It is no longer necessary, but it is an important link to their past.

Directions: Answer these questions about sign language.

1. Circle the main idea:

   (Native Americans used a kind of sign language.) [circled]

   There are many ways to express your thoughts to others.

2. Every tribe had its own sign language. True **(False)**
3. The Plains tribe did not use sign language. True **(False)**
4. Many Native Americans today still use this sign language. **(True)** False
5. Sign language is still necessary among Native Americans. True **(False)**

72

Reading Comprehension: Mermaids

One of the most popular fantasy characters is the mermaid. Many different countries have stories about these lovely creatures, which are half woman and half fish. In these fables, the mermaid is always beautiful—except perhaps for her greenish skin and webbed fingers!

There are some stories about mermen, too. They are said to have fine torsos with big, strong muscles in their chests and arms. But they have the most ugly faces—eyes like a pig, red noses, green teeth and seaweed hair!

A famous fable told in Ireland tells about a mermaid who was said to have been seen nearly 1,400 years ago. The story says that she could be heard singing beneath the waters for many years. One day, some men rowed out and caught her with a net. They were surprised to learn that she had once been a little human girl. Her family had died in a flood. But she survived beneath the waves and gradually changed into a mermaid.

Directions: Answer these questions about story.

1. Which definition is correct for **fantasy**?
   ☒ from the imagination and not real ☐ real ☐ living in the sea
2. Which definition is correct for **fable**?
   ☐ a true story ☒ a made-up story ☐ a story about fish
3. Which definition is correct for **torso**?
   ☐ the head ☒ the upper body but not the head ☐ the lower body
4. Which definition is correct for **survived**?
   ☐ swam ☐ died ☒ continued to live

73

Reading Comprehension: Paul Bunyan

There is a certain kind of fable called a "tall tale." In these stories, each storyteller tries to "top" the other. The stories get more and more unbelievable. A popular hero of American tall tales is Paul Bunyan—a giant of a man. Here are some of the stories that have been told about him.

Even as a baby, Paul was very big. One night, he rolled over in his sleep and knocked down a mile of trees. Of course, Paul's father wanted to find some way to keep Paul from getting hurt in his sleep and to keep him from knocking down all the forests. So he cut down some tall trees and made a boat for Paul to use as a cradle. He tied a long rope to the boat and let it drift out a little way into the sea to rock Paul to sleep.

One night, Paul had trouble sleeping. He kept turning over in his bed. Each time he turned, the cradle rocked. And each time the cradle rocked, it sent up waves as big as buildings. The waves got bigger and bigger until the people on the land were afraid they would all be drowned. They told Paul's parents that Paul was a danger to the whole state! So Paul and his parents had to move away.

After that, Paul didn't get into much trouble when he was growing up. His father taught him some very important lessons, such as, "If there are any towns or farms in your way, be sure to step around them!"

Directions: Answer these questions about Paul Bunyan.

1. What kind of fable is the story of Paul Bunyan? tall tale
2. What did Paul's father make for Paul to use as a cradle? boat
3. What happened when Paul rolled over in his cradle? He knocked down a mile of trees.
4. What did Paul's father tell Paul to do to towns and farms that were in his way?
   Step around them!

74

Reading Comprehension: Paul Bunyan

When Paul Bunyan grew up, he was taller than other men—by about 50 feet or so! Because of his size, he could do almost anything. One of the things he did best was to cut down trees and turn them into lumber. With only four strokes of his axe, he could cut off all the branches and bark. After he turned all the trees for miles into these tall square posts, he tied a long rope to an axe head. Then he yelled, "T-I-M-B-E-R-R-R!" and swung the rope around in a huge circle. With every swing, 100 trees fell to the ground.

One cold winter day, Paul found a huge blue ox stuck in the snow. It was nearly frozen. Although it was only a baby, even Paul could hardly lift it. Paul took the ox home and cared for it. He named it Babe, and they became best friends. Babe was a big help to Paul when he was cutting down trees.

When Babe was full grown, it was hard to tell how big he was. There were no scales big enough to weigh him. Paul once measured the distance between Babe's eyes. It was the length of 42 axe handles!

Once Paul and Babe were working with other men to cut lumber. The job was very hard because the road was so long and winding. It was said that the road was so crooked that men starting home for camp would meet themselves coming back! Well, Paul hitched Babe to the end of that crooked road. Babe pulled and pulled. He pulled so hard that his eyes nearly turned pink. There was a loud snap. The first curve came out of the road and Babe pulled harder. Finally the whole road started to move. Babe pulled it completely straight!

Directions: Answer these questions about Paul Bunyan and Babe.

1. What was Paul Bunyan particularly good at doing? Cutting down trees
2. What did Paul find in the snow? a huge blue ox
3. How big was the distance between Babe's eyes? 42 axe handles
4. What did Babe do to the crooked road? He pulled it completely straight.

75

Reading Comprehension: Hummingbirds

Hummingbirds are very small birds. This tiny bird is quite an acrobat. Only a few birds, such as kingfishers and sunbirds, can hover, which means to stay in one place in the air. But no other bird can match the flying skills of the hummingbird. The hummingbird can hover, fly backward and fly upside down!

Hummingbirds got their name because their wings move very quickly when they fly. This causes a humming sound. Their wings move so fast that you can't see them at all. This takes a lot of energy. These little birds must have food about every 20 minutes to have enough strength to fly. Their favorite foods are insects and nectar. Nectar is the sweet water deep inside a flower. Hummingbirds use their long, thin bills to drink from flowers. When a hummingbird sips nectar, it hovers in front of a flower. It never touches the flower with its wings or feet.

Besides being the best at flying, the hummingbird is also one of the prettiest birds. Of all the birds in the world, the hummingbird's colors are among the brightest. Some are bright green with red and white markings. Some are purple. One kind of hummingbird can change its color from reddish-brown to purple to red!

The hummingbird's nest is special, too. It looks like a tiny cup. The inside of the nest is very soft. This is because one of the things the mother bird uses to build the nest is the silk from a spider's web.

Directions: Answer these questions about hummingbirds.

1. How did hummingbirds get their name? Because their wings move very quickly when they fly, and it causes a humming sound.
2. What does **hover** mean? to hang in the air
3. How often do hummingbirds need to eat? every 20 minutes
4. Name two things that hummingbirds eat. insects and nectar
5. What is one of the things a mother hummingbird uses to build her nest?
   silk from a spider's web

76

Reading Comprehension: Bats

Bats are the only mammals that can fly. They have wings made of thin skin stretched between long fingers. Bats can fly amazing distances. Some small bats have been known to fly more than 25 miles in one night.

Most bats eat insects or fruit. But some eat only fish, others only blood and still others the nectar and pollen of flowers that bloom at night. Bats are active only at night. They sleep during the day in caves or other dark places. At rest, they always hang with their heads down.

You may have heard the expression "blind as a bat." But bats are not blind. They don't, however, use their eyes to guide their flight or to find the insects they eat. A bat makes a high-pitched squeak, then waits for the echo to return to it. This echo tells it how far away an object is. This is often called the bat's sonar system. Using this system, a bat can fly through a dark cave without bumping into anything. Hundreds of bats can fly about in the dark without ever running into each other. They do not get confused by the squeaks of the other bats. They always recognize their own echoes.

Directions: Answer these questions about bats.

1. Bats are the only mammals that
   ☐ eat insects. ☒ fly. ☐ live in caves.
2. Most bats eat
   ☐ plants. ☐ other animals. ☒ fruits and insects.
3. Bats always sleep
   ☒ with their heads down. ☐ lying down. ☐ during the night.
4. Bats are blind. True (False)
5. Bats use a built-in sonar system to guide them. (True) False
6. Bats are confused by the squeaks of other bats. True (False)

77

Reading Comprehension: Echoes

An echo is the repeating of a sound when it is reflected off a surface. For example, if you shout at a solid stone wall, your words often come back to you. This is your echo.

All sounds are made up of vibrations—very quick movements of the air. These vibrations move out in "sound waves." When a sound wave hits a hard, smooth surface, it is bent back. A rough surface breaks up the sound waves. In a valley with mountains all around, a sound may be echoed many times.

To experiment with echoes, stand at least 60 feet from the wall you will send the sound against. If you are any closer, the echo comes back too quickly. You would not be able to hear it as a separate sound because it would be mixed up with the original sound.

Directions: Answer these questions about echoes.

1. An echo occurs when sound waves are reflected off a surface. (True) False
2. Sounds are caused by vibrations of the air. (True) False
3. When sound hits a rough surface, it is bent back. True (False)
4. Sounds do not echo very well in a valley. True (False)
5. You must stand very close to a wall if you want to hear your echo. True (False)
6. What happens when a sound wave hits a hard, smooth surface?
   it is bent back
7. How far away must you stand from a wall if you want to experiment with echoes?
   at least 60 feet
8. Which word in the story means to try something as a test? experiment
9. What are vibrations? very quick movements of the air

78

Reading Comprehension: Chameleons

Chameleons (ka-MEAL-yens) are the strangest of all lizards. They can change their colors among greens, browns, reds, yellows, white and black. This helps them hide. They can become the color of whatever they are standing next to.

Chameleons range in size from 1 1/2 inches to 2 feet. They have very long tongues and long tails that can grab onto things. As lizards, chameleons are members of the reptile family. Many reptiles, such as the snake, can move very fast. But chameleons move very, very slowly. They move one leg at a time and creep along as though they are afraid they will fall down.

All reptiles can move their eyes independently. That means they can look in different directions with each eye. This is very easy to see on the chameleon. The chameleon's eye is almost completely covered by the eyelid, with only a tiny hole in the middle when their eyes are open. The hole moves as the eye moves. You might see a chameleon with one eye pointing up and the other one pointing down.

A chameleon's tongue is longer than its head and body put together. It has a large, sticky spot on the end. When a chameleon sees an insect, he shoots his tongue out, catches it and then snaps his tongue back into his mouth and swallows the insect.

Directions: Answer these questions about chameleons.

1. A chameleon can change its colors.
2. Chameleons belong to the family of reptiles.
3. As with all reptiles, the chameleon can move its eyes independently.
4. A chameleon's tongue is longer than
   ☐ its head. ☐ its body. ☒ its head and body put together.
5. A chameleon eats
   ☒ insects. ☐ fruit. ☐ nectar.

79

Reading Comprehension: The Solar System

You live on a planet—the planet Earth. It is one of nine planets that follows an orbit around the Sun. The other eight planets are Mercury, Venus, Mars, Jupiter, Saturn, Uranus, Neptune and Pluto. These nine planets are part of the solar system. The word **sol**, the ootbase word for **solar**, means sun. The Sun is at the center of the solar system and is very important. So, you could call the solar system the "Sun System."

You can see some of the planets by looking at the sky on a clear night. Mercury, Venus, Mars, Jupiter and Saturn look like bright stars. You need a telescope to see Uranus, Neptune and Pluto because they are not very bright. These planets are the most distant in the solar system.

The Moon is also part of the solar system. Just as Earth circles around the Sun in an orbit, the Moon circles Earth. This is why it is often called Earth's satellite. Most of the other planets have satellites, too. Jupiter has 16 moons! You need a telescope to see them.

Directions: Answer these questions about the solar system.

1. Which definition is correct for **orbit**?
   ☐ planet ☒ path ☐ moon
2. Which definition is correct for **telescope**?
   ☒ an instrument that makes distant objects seem closer and larger
   ☐ a flashlight
   ☐ an instrument to measure the size of planets
3. Which definition is correct for **satellite**?
   ☒ a small heavenly body in an orbit around a bigger one
   ☐ a path
   ☐ a solar system

82

Reading Comprehension: Planet Facts

It takes Earth 365 days—one year—to complete one orbit around the Sun. Mercury, the planet closest to the Sun, takes only 88 days to orbit the Sun. But Pluto takes about 248 years!

Because they are the farthest from the Sun, Neptune and Pluto are the coldest planets. Their temperatures are about 370 degrees below zero! Mercury and Venus are the hottest planets. The temperature can reach 620 degrees on Mercury and 882 degrees on Venus. Plants and animals cannot live on these planets because they would either freeze or burn up. In fact, scientists believe that Earth is the only planet in our solar system where plants, animals and people can live. This is why Earth is called the "living planet."

Earth is a middle-sized planet. Four of the planets are smaller than Earth. They are Mercury, Venus, Mars and Pluto. Jupiter, Saturn, Uranus and Neptune are all larger than Earth. Jupiter is the biggest planet. It is more than 1,000 times bigger than Earth. Pluto is the smallest planet. Earth is about four times bigger than Pluto.

The Sun is really a star. Stars are balls of hot, glowing gas. The Sun looks so much bigger than the other stars because it is so much closer. It is only 93 million miles away from Earth. The next closest star is 25 trillion miles away!

Directions: Answer these questions about the planets.

1. How many days does it take Earth to orbit the Sun? 365 days
2. Which are the two coldest planets? Neptune and Pluto
3. Which are the two hottest planets? Mercury and Venus
4. What is Earth sometimes called? the living planet
5. Which planets are bigger than Earth? Jupiter, Saturn, Uranus and Neptune
6. What is a star? a ball of hot, glowing gas

83

Reading Comprehension: Planet Facts

Directions: Read about the planets. Then unscramble the name of each planet and write it on the line.

1. **peNnute** takes 165 years to complete its path, or orbit, around the Sun. Neptune
2. **piteJur** has 16 moons orbiting around it. Jupiter
3. **oPult** is the coldest planet—400 degrees below zero! Pluto
4. **sarM** is nicknamed the "red planet." Mars
5. **aruntS** is one of the most beautiful planets to look at through a telescope because of the many rings that surround it. Saturn
6. **cryMure** is the planet closest to the Sun. Mercury
7. **rathE** is sometimes called the "living planet." Earth
8. Until recent discoveries, **seVun** was thought of as the "mystery planet" because it is covered by thick clouds. Venus
9. **rUsanu** rotates lying on its side. Uranus

84

Reading Comprehension: Mars and Earth

Earth is the only planet that scientists are certain has life. What does Earth have that the other planets don't? For one thing, Earth is just the right temperature. As the third planet from the sun, Earth seems to be just the right distance away. The planets closer to the Sun are so hot that their surfaces bake. The farthest planets are frozen balls.

When Earth developed—which scientists believe may have happened about 4 billion years ago—many gases covered the planet. These gases caused Earth to be hot. But the temperature was just right for thick clouds to form. It rained very hard for a very long time. This gave Earth its oceans. Water made it possible for plants to grow. The plants created oxygen in the atmosphere. Oxygen is the gas that humans and animals breathe.

Only one other planet in the solar system seems to be anything like Earth. That planet is Mars. Mars is smaller than Earth, and it is quite a bit cooler. But it is not too cold for humans. On some days, the temperatures are as cold as a winter day in the northern United States. If you wore a special space suit, you could walk around on Mars. You would have to bring your own air to breathe, because the air on Mars is too thin.

Mars has the largest volcano in the solar system. It is 16 miles high. The highest volcano on Earth is 5 miles high. The most unexpected sights on Mars are dried-up riverbeds. Scientists believe that Mars was once much wetter. Does this mean there could have been living things on Mars? Scientists are not sure, but there has been no sign so far.

Directions: Answer these questions about Mars and Earth.

1. Name three things Earth has that makes life possible.
   right temperature b. water c. oxygen
2. According to scientists, how long ago did Earth develop? 4 billion years
3. What planet is most like Earth? Mars
4. Mars has the biggest volcano in the solar system. How tall is it? 16 miles
5. Why can't you breathe on Mars? The air is too thin.

85

Reading Comprehension: The Moon

Earth has a partner in its trip around the Sun. It is the Moon. The Moon is Earth's satellite. It moves around Earth very quickly. It takes the Moon 28 days to go around Earth one time.

While they are partners in the solar system, the Earth and the Moon are very different. Earth is filled with life. It is a very colorful planet. The Moon is gray and lifeless. Nothing can live on the Moon.

There is no air on the Moon. Astronauts must wear special space suits when they walk on the Moon so they can breathe. The moon also has no water. There is no weather, so the sky above the Moon always looks black.

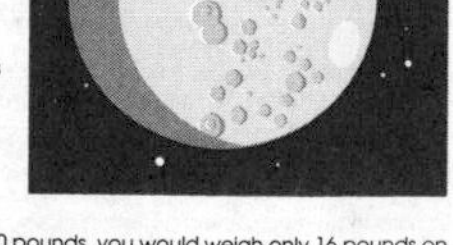

You would not weigh as much on the Moon as you do on Earth. If you weigh 100 pounds, you would weigh only 16 pounds on the Moon. It is very different to walk on the Moon, too. You would bounce and float!

Directions: Answer these questions about the Moon.

1. What is Earth's partner in the solar system? the Moon
2. How long does it take the Moon to go around Earth? 28 days
3. There is no life on the Moon. (True) False
4. There is lots of water on the Moon. True (False)
5. You would weigh more on the Moon than you do on Earth. True (False)

86

Reading Comprehension: Constellations

Constellations are pictures in the sky. The pictures are made of stars. There are 88 constellations in all. Some pictures are of animals from ancient Greek stories, such as horses that fly. There are also brave heroes and terrible monsters. The constellations are hard to find at first, but with practice, you can locate them.

The most famous star picture is called Ursa Major. This means "the Great Bear." There are many stars in this picture, but the seven stars that make up the body are very bright and easy to see. They look like a giant pan. You may have heard of this picture by its more common name—the Big Dipper. There is another constellation called Ursa Minor. It also is shaped like a pan, and is called the Little Dipper.

There is a group of 12 constellations called the Zodiac. They are lined up one after another all around the sky. Each month, a different member of the Zodiac rises in the east. Each day, more of it becomes visible. After 1 year, the entire picture has been overhead. Most of the pictures of the Zodiac are animals, including Taurus the bull and Scorpius the scorpion. The Scorpius is the biggest constellation in the Zodiac. There are pictures of people, too, such as Sagittarius, the archer, with his big bow and arrow.

Directions: Answer these questions about constellations.

1. What is a constellation? a picture in the sky
2. How many constellations are there? 12
3. What is the more common name for Ursa Major? the Big Dipper
4. What is the name for the group of 12 constellations lined up around the sky? the Zodiac
5. What is the biggest constellation in the Zodiac? Scorpius

87

Reading Comprehension: Telescopes

A telescope is an instrument that makes distant objects, such as the stars and planets, seem closer and bigger. This allows us to get a better look at them and scientists to learn more about them. In 1990, a very special telescope was launched into the sky aboard the space shuttle *Discovery*. The Hubble Space Telescope (HST), which is named for the man who invented it, cost almost 2 billion dollars to make.

HST is a powerful eye in the sky that may help answer questions scientists have asked for a long time: How did the universe begin? How will it end? Is there other life in the universe?

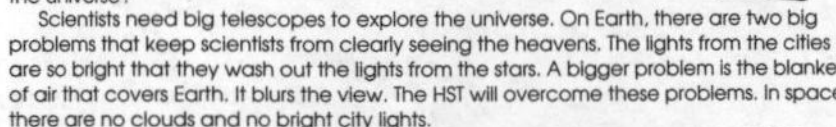

Scientists need big telescopes to explore the universe. On Earth, there are two big problems that keep scientists from clearly seeing the heavens. The lights from the cities are so bright that they wash out the lights from the stars. A bigger problem is the blanket of air that covers Earth. It blurs the view. The HST will overcome these problems. In space there are no clouds and no bright city lights.

The HST is a huge telescope. It is 43 feet long and 14 feet across. It weighs 24,250 pounds. It is very powerful, too. Scientists say that if you put a dime on the top of the Washington Monument in Washington, D.C., you would be able to clearly read the date on it from New York City using the HST. That is 175 miles away!

Directions: Answer these questions about a special telescope.

1. What is a telescope? an instrument that makes distant objects seem closer and bigger
2. What is the name of the giant telescope that was launched into space in 1990? The Hubble Space Telescope
3. What are two problems for scientists trying to look at the stars and planets from Earth? Lights from cities wash out stars, and the air blurs vision
4. How much does the HST weigh? 24,250 pounds

88

Space Pioneer

Neil Armstrong is one of the great pioneers of space. On July 20, 1969, Armstrong was commander of *Apollo 11*, the first manned American spacecraft to land on the Moon. He was the first person to walk on the Moon.

Armstrong was born in Ohio in 1930. He took his first airplane ride when he was 6 years old. As he grew older, he did jobs to earn money to learn to fly. On his 16th birthday, he received his student pilot's license.

Armstrong served as a Navy fighter pilot during the Korean War. He received three medals. Later, he was a test pilot. He was known as one of the best pilots in the world. He was also an engineer. He contributed much to the development of new methods of flying. In 1962, he was into an astronaut training program.

Armstrong had much experience when he was named to command the historic flight to the Moon. It took four days to fly to the Moon. As he climbed down the ladder to be the first person to step onto the Moon, he said these now famous words: "That's one small step for man, one giant leap for mankind."

Directions: Answer these questions about Neil Armstrong.

1. What did Neil Armstrong do before any other person in the world? He walked on the Moon.
2. How old was Neil Armstrong when he got his student pilot's license? 16 years old
3. What did Armstrong do during the Korean War? served as a Navy fighter pilot
4. On what date did a person first walk on the Moon? July 20, 1969

89

Reading Comprehension: Amelia Earhart

More than 35 years before Neil Armstrong took that first step onto the surface of the Moon, another pioneer of the sky was becoming famous. Amelia Earhart was the first woman to fly around the world alone. She performed this amazing feat in 1932—2 years after Neil Armstrong was born.

Amelia saw an airplane for the first time at a fair when she was 8 years old. She was disappointed by the experience. She never would have dreamed that one day she would be a great pilot. Amelia didn't take her first plane ride for many years after that. But her first flight convinced her that she wanted to learn to fly. Her flying teacher, Neta Snook, was one of very few women at the time who knew how to fly. This inspired Amelia to learn to fly.

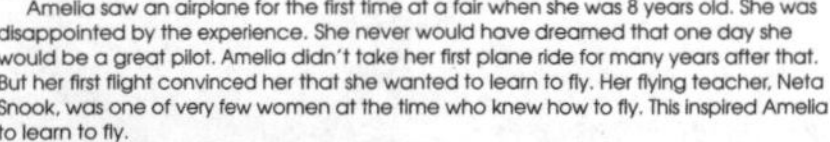

In 1927, she read about a man named Charles Lindbergh who became the first person to fly across the Atlantic Ocean alone. This was very dangerous at that time. In 1928, Amelia was a crew member of a plane that flew across the ocean. She was the first woman to do this. Four years later she made the trip on her own.

Amelia was very famous. The president called her an American heroine. Then, in 1937, Amelia decided to try to fly around the world at the equator. This had never been done before. Amelia never returned from the trip. To this day, no one knows for sure what happened to her. Many believe that she crashed into the ocean. But her failure was a challenge to others. She was indeed a great pioneer of the sky.

Directions: Answer these questions about Amelia Earhart.

1. What is the correct definition for **feat**?
   - [x] achievement
   - [ ] trick
   - [ ] flight
2. What is the correct definition for **inspired**?
   - [ ] discouraged
   - [x] made to want to do
   - [ ] frightened
3. How did Amelia Earhart feel the first time she saw an airplane? disappointed
4. Name the two things that Amelia Earhart was the first woman to achieve.
   a. flew across the Atlantic Ocean
   b. flew around the world alone

90

Reading Comprehension: Volcanoes

The volcano is one of the most amazing and frightening forces of nature. Maybe you have seen pictures of these "fireworks" of nature. Sometimes when a volcano erupts, a huge wall of melted rock creeps down its sides. It looks like a river of fire. Sometimes volcanoes explode, throwing the melted rock and ashes high into the air. But where does this melted rock come from?

The Earth is made up of many layers. The top layer is called the crust. Under the crust are many layers of hard rock. But far, far beneath the crust is rock so hot that it is soft. In some places it even melts. The melted rock is called magma. Sometimes the magma breaks out to the surface through cracks in the crust. These cracks are volcanoes.

Most people think of mountains when they think of volcanoes. But not every mountain is a volcano. A volcano is simply the opening in the earth from which the magma escapes. The hot magma, or lava cools and builds up on the surface of the Earth. Over thousands of years, this pile of cooled lava can grow to be very, very big. For example, the highest mountain in Africa, Kilimanjaro, is a volcano. It towers more than 16,000 feet above the ground around it.

Directions: Answer these questions about volcanoes.

1. What is the correct definition for **erupts**?
   - [ ] drips out
   - [x] bursts out
   - [ ] seeps out
2. What is the correct definition for **layer**?
   - [ ] rocks
   - [x] a single thickness
   - [ ] ground
3. What is the top layer of the earth called? crust
4. What is the word for hot magma that spills out of the Earth? lava
5. Where is the volcano called Kilimanjaro located? Africa

91

Reading Comprehension: Oceans

If you looked at Earth from up in space, you would see a planet that is mostly blue. This is because more than two-thirds of Earth is covered with water. You already know that this is what makes our planet different from the others, and what makes life on Earth possible. Most of this water is in the four great oceans: Pacific, Atlantic, Indian and Arctic. The Pacific is by far the largest and the deepest. It is more than twice as big as the Atlantic, the second largest ocean.

The water in the ocean is salty. This is because rivers are always pouring water into the oceans. Some of this water picks up salt from the rocks it flows over. It is not enough salt to make the rivers taste salty. But the salt in the oceans has been building up over millions of years. The oceans get more and more salty every century.

The ocean provides us with huge amounts of food, especially fish. There are many other things we get from the ocean, including sponges and pearls. The oceans are also great "highways" of the world. Ships are always crossing the oceans, transporting many goods from country to country.

The science of studying the ocean is called oceanography. Today, oceanographers have special equipment to help them learn about the oceans and seas. Electronic instruments can be sent deep below the surface to make measurements. The newest equipment uses sonar or echo-sounding systems that bounce sound waves off the sea bed and use the echoes to make pictures of the ocean floor.

Directions: Answer these questions about the oceans.

1. How much of the Earth is covered by water? two-thirds
2. Which is the largest and deepest ocean? Pacific
3. What is the science of studying the ocean? oceanography
4. What new equipment do oceanographers use? sonar or echo sounding systems

92

Reading Comprehension: Whales

The biggest animal in the world is the whale. The blue whale is the largest animal that ever lived. It is even bigger than the great dinosaurs of long ago. Whales are close cousins to dolphins and porpoises, but these animals are fewer than 13 feet in length.

Whales spend their entire lives in water, usually in the ocean. Because of this, many people think that whales are fish. They are not. They are mammals. There are four things that prove that whales are mammals instead of fish: 1) Whales breathe with lungs instead of gills. A whale must come to the surface to breathe. It blows the old air from its lungs out of a hole in the top of its head. 2) They are warm-blooded. 3) They have hair—though not very much! 4) Baby whales are born alive and get milk from their mothers.

Because whales often live in cold water, they have a thick layer of fat under their skin to protect them. This fat is called blubber. For many centuries, people have hunted the whale for its blubber.

Whales are very sociable animals and "talk" with each other by making different noises, including clicks, whistles, squeaks, thumps and low moans. Because sound waves travel well in water, the "song" of some whales can be heard more than 100 miles away.

Directions: Answer these questions about whales.

1. Which whale is the biggest animal that has ever lived? blue whale
2. List four things proving that whales are mammals and not fish.
   a. They breathe air.
   b. They are warm-blooded.
   c. They have hair.
   d. The babies are born alive and get milk from their mother.
3. What are two "cousins" to the whale? dolphins and porpoises
4. What is the thick layer of fat under a whale's skin called? blubber

93

Reading Comprehension: Dolphins and Porpoises

Dolphins and porpoises are members of the whale family. In fact, they are the most common whales. If they have pointed or "beaked" faces, they are dolphins. If they have short faces, they are porpoises. Sometimes large groups of more than 1,000 dolphins can be seen.

Dolphins and porpoises swim in a special way called "porpoising." They swim through the surface waters, diving down and then leaping up—sometimes into the air. As their heads come out of the water, they breathe in air. Dolphins are acrobatic swimmers, often spinning in the air as they leap.

Humans have always had a special relationship with dolphins. Stories dating back to the ancient Greeks talk about dolphins as friendly, helpful creatures. There have been reports over the years of people in trouble on the seas who have been rescued and helped by dolphins.

Directions: Answer these questions about dolphins and porpoises.

1. The small members of the whale family with the pointed faces are dolphins.
2. Those members of the whale family with short faces are porpoises.
3. What do you call the special way dolphins and porpoises swim? porpoising.
4. Do dolphins breathe with lungs or gills? lungs
5. How did ancient Greeks describe dolphins? friendly, helpful creatures
6. Where have dolphins been reported to help people? in trouble on the seas

94

Reading Comprehension: Sharks

Sharks are known as the hunters of the sea. They are fish who eat other fish and even other sharks. Most people are frightened of sharks, but only a few of the more than 300 types of sharks are dangerous to people. Sharks vary in size and shape. The whale shark can be up to 60 feet long, but it is harmless. Some kinds of dogfish sharks are only a few inches long!

Sharks usually live in warm water, although they can be found anywhere in the ocean. Because of their shape, they are great swimmers.

Sharks are different from most other fish in a few ways. One important way is that they don't have any bones. Instead, their bodies have tough material called cartilage. Another way sharks are different is that their mouths are on the underside of the head. Most sharks have several rows of very sharp teeth. They never stop growing teeth. If a tooth wears out or is lost, a new one grows in its place.

Sharks spend most of their time eating and looking for food. They are excellent hunters. They can smell the smallest amount of blood from a long way off. Some kinds of sharks swim in packs, but the larger sharks hunt alone. Sharks usually approach their prey carefully, especially if it is big. Unless they are very hungry, they will swim around in a circle for some time before attacking. Experienced divers know how to swim with sharks and feed them. They can tell by the way a shark comes up to them if they should be afraid.

Directions: Answer these questions about sharks.

1. Sharks are the hunters of the sea.	(True)	False
2. There are thousands of kinds of sharks.	True	(False)
3. All sharks are dangerous to humans.	True	(False)
4. Sharks actually have very few teeth.	True	(False)
5. Sharks spend most of their time eating and looking for food.	(True)	False

95

Reading Comprehension: Jacques Cousteau

Jacques Cousteau was one of the most famous undersea explorers in history. He revolutionized this study with his inventions. His inventions include the aqua-lung and the diving saucer.

Jacques-Yves Cousteau was born in France in 1910. His family traveled a lot when he was a boy. They often visited the Atlantic Ocean. Even then, he was developing what would become a lifelong love for the sea.

Because of all the moving his family did, Cousteau was a poor student in school. He was often in trouble. But there were some areas in which he did very well. He was a wonderful swimmer, and he loved to invent things. Even as a teenager, he invented things that amazed grown-ups. He also learned a lot about other languages. By the time he started college, he was one of the best students in school. Because of his good grades, he was able to go to the French Naval Academy.

During World War II, Cousteau served as an officer in the French Navy. Most of his life became centered around the sea. He dreamed of owning his own ship. Finally, in 1950, he bought the *Calypso* (ca-LIP-so) and turned it into a research ship. Cousteau and his sailors explored the oceans. They searched shipwrecks and made underwater movies. He eventually won three Academy Awards for his undersea films. He also wrote many books about sea life. He worked very hard to teach people about the sea and how to take are of it.

Directions: Complete these statements about Jacques Cousteau.

1. Jacques Cousteau was born in France.
2. As a boy, Cousteau liked to swim and to invent things.
3. Cousteau's ship was called Calypso.
4. Cousteau's undersea films won him three Academy Awards.

96

Reading Comprehension: Deep-Sea Diving

One part of the world is still largely unexplored. It is the deep sea. Over the years, many people have explored the sea. But the first deep-sea divers wanted to find sunken treasure. They weren't really interested in studying the creatures or life there. Only recently have they begun to learn some of the mysteries of the sea.

It's not easy to explore the deep sea. A diver must have a way of breathing under water. He must be able to protect himself from the terrific pressure. The pressure of air is about 15 pounds on every square inch. But the pressure of water is about 1,300 pounds on every square inch!

The first diving suits were made of rubber. They had a helmet of brass with windows in it. The shoes were made of lead and weighed 20 pounds each! These suits let divers go down a few hundred feet, but they were no good for exploring very deep waters. With a metal diving suit, a diver could go down 700 feet. Metal suits were first used in the 1930s.

In 1937, a diver named William Beebe wanted to explore deeper than anyone had ever gone before. He was not interested in finding treasure. He wanted to study deep-sea creatures and plants. He invented a hollow metal ball called the bathysphere. It weighed more than 5,000 pounds, but in it Beebe went down 3,028 feet. He saw many things that had never been seen by humans before.

Directions: Answer these questions about early deep-sea diving.

1. What were the first deep-sea divers interested in? sunken treasure
2. What are two problems that must be overcome in deep-sea diving?
   a. the terrific air pressure
   b. breathing under water
3. How deep could a diver go wearing a metal suit? 700 feet
4. Who was the deep-sea explorer who invented the bathysphere? William Beebe

97

Reading Comprehension: Occupations

Directions: Read this article about coaching. Then answer the questions below.

When you see your coach at the practice field or in a game, you are seeing only a small part of your coach's life. Your coach has to spend a great deal of time even before your season begins. He/she needs to attend meetings so that the teams can be divided into groups. Each coach in the conference (a group of teams that are scheduled to play each other) has to attend more meetings—this time to set up the dates they will have games.

Your coach, whether it is a man or a woman, usually has a job to go to every day. The time he/she spends with you and your team mates means that he/she has even less time to spend with friends and family. Your coach feels it is important to help you learn how to play and to learn good sportsmanship.

The next time you sign up for a sport, look at your coach with a "different set of eyes." Always do your best, be a good team player and remember to thank your coach for all that he/she does!

1. What is a conference? a group of teams scheduled to play each other
2. What does it mean to look at your coach with a "different set of eyes"? He/she usually has another job to go to everyday.
3. Name one way you can show your coach you appreciate him/her. Thank him/her for all he/she does.

98

Reading Comprehension: Occupations

Directions: Read this story about artistic people. Then answer the questions below.

Are you a good artist? Do you like to draw? Some people like to sit and "doodle" when they are listening to the radio, watching television or talking on the telephone. You might have noticed these little cartoons or designs written on the message pad by your phone. (The "doodler" has been here!)

It is true that people like their occupations better if they are doing something they enjoy. It would not be much fun to be a great artist and have to work as a bus driver or a store clerk. These are some of the jobs you could have if you were a good artist: book illustrator, greeting card artist, art teacher, movie animator, cartoonist for magazines or newspapers.

1. What is a "doodler"? Someone who draws while doing other things.
2. Read the list of five possible occupations for an artist. Pretend you are an artist. Which job would you choose? Why? book illustrator, art teacher, movie animator, cartoonist, greeting card artist Reasons will vary.

99

Reading Skills: Advertisements

Stores pay for advertisements, or ads, to let people know what is being sold. You see ads in newspapers and magazines, and on television and radio.

Directions: Use the following newspaper ad to answer the questions.

Home Cooking Restaurant

Open Easter Sunday 10:30 a.m. to 8:00 p.m.

Special Easter Menu
- Roast Turkey $10.50
- Baked Ham $12.00
- Roast Leg of Lamb $15.50

Many other dishes available, including veal, chicken, seafood and pasta.

Call for reservations 555–6241

Home Cooking Restaurant
1485 City Street

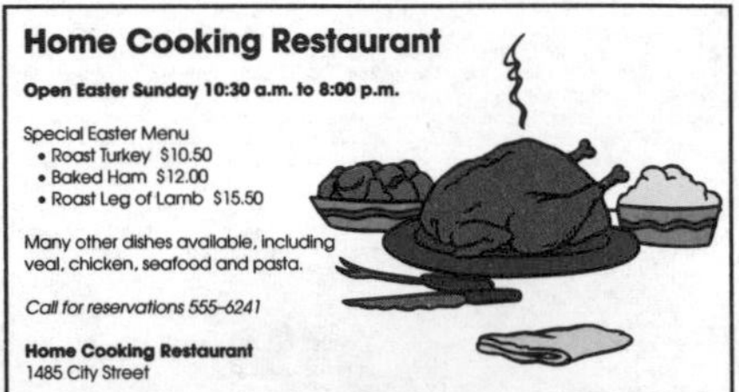

1. The restaurant is advertising special holiday meals. What holiday are they for? Easter
2. What is the most expensive meal listed on the menu? roast leg of lamb
3. What hours will the restaurant be open on Easter? 10:30 a.m. to 8:00 p.m.

100

Reading Skills: Advertisements

Directions: Use the following newspaper ad to answer the questions.

New-Look Fashions

Final Week!
Spring Suit Sale

Buy one suit at the regular price and get a second one for only $50!

Suits: From $75 to $150

New-Look Fashions
5290 Main Street

Hours: Monday–Friday 10–7; Saturday 10–6; Closed Sunday

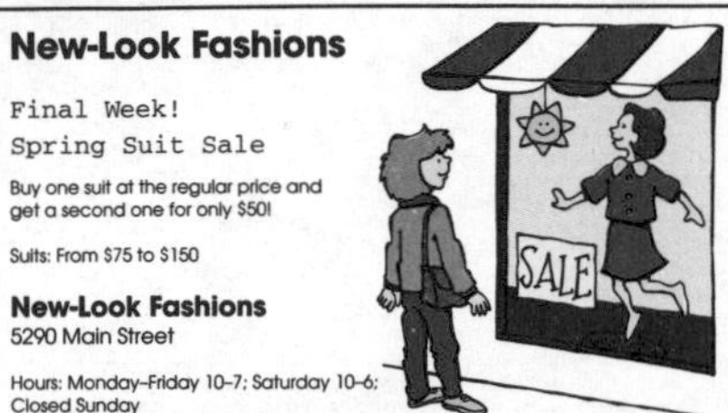

1. What is the regular price for a suit? $75 to $150
2. If you buy one suit at the regular price, what is the price for a second one? $50
3. What day is the store closed? Sunday
4. What hours is the store open on Wednesday? between 10 a.m. and 7 p.m.
5. When is the sale? this week

101

Reading Skills: Advertisements

Directions: Use the following newspaper ad to answer the questions.

House of Plants

Colorful Flowering Trees

Flowering Crab Apple Trees
Sizes up to 10 ft.
Beautiful Colored Spring Flowers
Dark Green Foliage
Red, Pink, White Blossoms

25% OFF

Reg. $29.99 to $149.99
NOW $22.49 to $112.50

House of Plants
6280 River Road

1. How big are the biggest flowering crab apple trees for sale? Up to 10 feet
2. What are the regular prices? $29.99 to $149.99
3. What are the sale prices? $22.49 to $112.50

102

Reading Skills: Bus Schedules

Schedules are important to our daily lives. Your parents' jobs, school, even watching television—all are based on schedules. When you travel, you probably follow a schedule, too. Most forms of public transportation, such as subways, buses and trains, run on schedules. These "timetables" tell passengers when they will leave each stop or station.

Directions: Use the following city bus schedule to answer the questions.

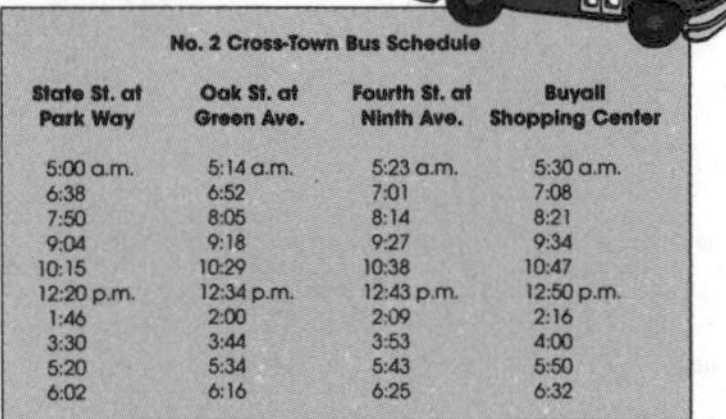

No. 2 Cross-Town Bus Schedule

State St. at Park Way	Oak St. at Green Ave.	Fourth St. at Ninth Ave.	Buyall Shopping Center
5:00 a.m.	5:14 a.m.	5:23 a.m.	5:30 a.m.
6:38	6:52	7:01	7:08
7:50	8:05	8:14	8:21
9:04	9:18	9:27	9:34
10:15	10:29	10:38	10:47
12:20 p.m.	12:34 p.m.	12:43 p.m.	12:50 p.m.
1:46	2:00	2:09	2:16
3:30	3:44	3:53	4:00
5:20	5:34	5:43	5:50
6:02	6:16	6:25	6:32

1. The first bus of the day leaves the State St./Park Way stop at 5 a.m. What time does the last bus of the day leave this stop? 6:02 p.m.
2. The bus that leaves the Oak St./Green Ave. stop at 8:05 a.m. leaves the Buyall Shopping Center at what time? 8:21 a.m.
3. What time does the first afternoon bus leave the Fourth St./Ninth Ave. stop? 12:43 p.m.
4. How many buses each day run between the State St./Park Way stop and the Buyall Shopping Center? 10

103

Reading Skills: Train Schedules

Directions: Below is part of a schedule for trains leaving New York City for cities all around the country. Use the schedule to answer the questions.

Destination	Train Number	Departure Time	Arrival Time
Birmingham	958	9:00 a.m.	12:31 a.m.
Boston	611	7:15 a.m.	4:30 p.m.
Cambridge	398	8:15 a.m.	1:14 p.m.
Cincinnati	242	5:00 a.m.	7:25 p.m.
Detroit	415	1:45 p.m.	4:40 a.m.
Evansville	623	3:00 p.m.	8:28 a.m.

1. What is the number of the train that leaves latest in the day? 623
2. What city is the destination for train number 623? Evansville
3. What time does the train for Boston leave New York? 7:15 a.m.
4. What time does train number 415 arrive in Detroit? 4:40 a.m.
5. What is the destination of the train that leaves earliest in the day? Cincinnati

104

Reading Skills: Labels

Directions: You should never take any medicine without your parents' permission, but it is good to know how to read the label of a medicine bottle. Read the label to answer the questions.

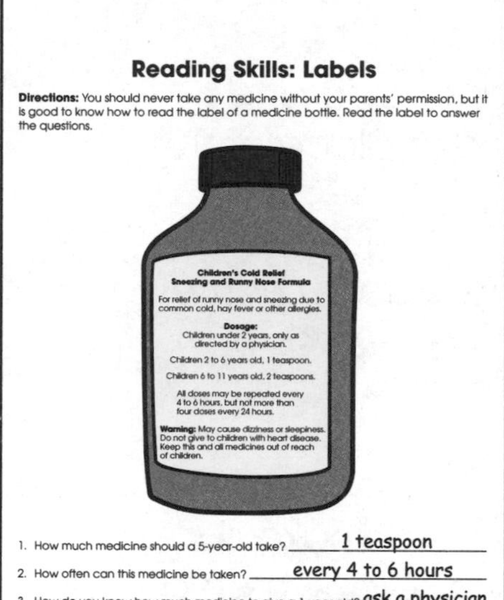

Children's Cold Relief
Sneezing and Runny Nose Formula
For relief of runny nose and sneezing due to common cold, hay fever or other allergies.
Dosage:
Children under 2 years, only as directed by a physician.
Children 2 to 6 years old, 1 teaspoon.
Children 6 to 11 years old, 2 teaspoons.
All doses may be repeated every 4 to 6 hours, but not more than four doses every 24 hours.
Warning: May cause dizziness or sleepiness. Do not give to children with heart disease. Keep this and all medicines out of reach of children.

1. How much medicine should a 5-year-old take? 1 teaspoon
2. How often can this medicine be taken? every 4 to 6 hours
3. How do you know how much medicine to give a 1-year-old? ask a physician
4. Who should not take this medicine? children with heart disease

105

Reading Skills: Labels

Directions: Use the following medicine bottle label to answer the questions.

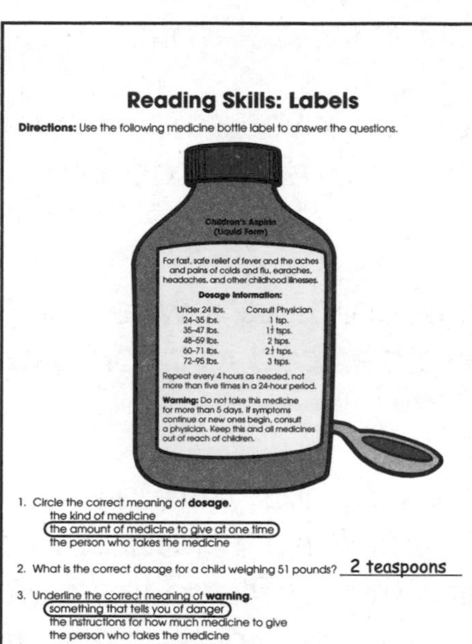

1. Circle the correct meaning of **dosage**.
   - the kind of medicine
   - the amount of medicine to give at one time
   - the person who takes the medicine
2. What is the correct dosage for a child weighing 51 pounds? 2 teaspoons
3. Underline the correct meaning of **warning**.
   - something that tells you of danger
   - the instructions for how much medicine to give
   - the person who takes the medicine

106

Review

Directions: Use the following "Help Wanted" ads to answer the questions.

Baby-sitter. Caring, responsible person needed to take care of 2 and 4 year old in our home. 25–30 hours per week. Must have own transportation. References required. Call 725-1342 after 7 p.m.

Clerk/Typist. Law firm seeks part-time help. Duties include typing, filing and answering telephone. Monday–Friday, 1–6 p.m. Previous experience preferred. Apply in person. 1392 E. Long St.

Driver for Disabled. Van provided. Includes some evenings and Saturdays. No experience necessary. Call Mike at 769-1533.

Head Nurse. Join in the bloodmobile team at the American Red Cross. Full- and part-time positions available. Great benefits. Apply Monday thru Friday 9–4. 1495 N. State St.

Teachers. For new child-care program. Prefer degree in Early Childhood Development and previous experience. Must be non-smoker. Call 291-5555.

1. For which job would you have to work some evenings and Saturdays? Driver for Disabled
2. Which job calls for a person who does not smoke? Teacher
3. For which job would you have to have your own transportation? Baby-sitter
4. For which job must you apply in person? Clerk/Typist
5. Which ad offers both part-time and full-time positions? Head Nurse

107

Teaching Suggestions

Vocabulary Building

Encourage your child to learn a new word each week. He/she should learn its meaning and use it when applicable throughout the week. You may select the word from those your child brings home from his/her science, math, reading, spelling or social studies school work.

Be aware of words your child may overuse in his/her language and writing. Decide together on synonyms that can be used in place of the overused words.

Buy a thesaurus and help your child use it when he/she is doing homework. This handy reference can also be used to decide on new "words of the week."

Play a matching game with your child. Write new vocabulary words on pieces of tagboard cut into playing-card size. For each word card, make a definition card (synonym, antonym, and so on). Place the cards face down on a table. Turn over two cards at a time to see if they match. If they don't match, the next player tries to locate a match.

Classifying

Play a game with your child to help him/her understand classifying. Tell your child three or four related words (oak, pine, elm, maple). Then ask him/her to tell you the group in which they belong (trees). If your child has trouble doing this mental activity, write the words on strips of paper and have your child place them under headings you have provided.

Invite your child to give you groups of objects to place under headings. If your child can name several things that belong together, then he/she probably understands the concept. Your child may find that it is harder to come up with the words than it is to place them in the correct group, so use this as a challenge activity.

Following Directions/Sequencing

By fourth grade, your child should be able to listen carefully and follow directions. Before your child begins an activity, remind him/her to read carefully and make sure he/she understands the directions.

Make a favorite recipe together. Your child will benefit from spending the time with you—not just in creating a good dessert but in the time spent together! Explain to your child why ingredients must be mixed in a certain order and why some steps must be done before others.

Point out that sequencing can also be applied to writing or retelling a story.

Remind your child that letters have to be in a certain order to make words, words have to be in a certain order to make sentences that make sense and paragraphs and story events have to be in a certain order.

Create a game with written clues that direct your child to new clues. A series of clues followed correctly could lead to the ice-cream shop, video store or a special treat!

Reading and Comprehension

When you read to or with your child, discuss the details of the story. Ask questions to guide your child to understand something important that happened in the beginning, middle and end of the story. Many stories have a problem that needs to be solved or a situation that needs to be addressed. Discuss these details with your child to broaden his/her understanding.

Enhance your child's understanding of a story by encouraging him/her to "picture in his/her head" what the characters look like or how a scene looks as the author describes it.

Ask your child questions about the story before you begin reading. For example: "What do you think the people in this picture are doing?" "What do you think the title means?" "Do you think this will be a true story or a made-up story?" Then as your child reads, he/she will already be thinking about answers to these questions.